Customer service and distribution strategy

Customer service and distribution strategy

MARTIN CHRISTOPHER
PHILIP SCHARY
TAGE SKJOTT-LARSEN

A HALSTED PRESS BOOK

JOHN WILEY & SONS
New York — Toronto

5-2-91

English language edition, except USA and Canada published by
Associated Business Press, an imprint of
Associated Business Programmes Ltd
Ludgate House
107-111 Fleet Street
London EC4A 2AB

Published in USA and Canada by
Halsted Press, a division of John Wiley & Sons Inc
New York

First published 1979

Library of Congress Cataloguing in Publication Data

Christopher, Martin
   Customer service and distribution strategy

"A Halsted Press book."

Includes index.

1. Customer service. I. Schary, Philip B., joint author.
II. Skjott-Larsen, Tage, joint author. III. Title.
HF5415.5.C48   658.8'12   79-24121

ISBN 0-470-26890-5

© Copyright Martin Christopher, Philip Schary & Tage Skjott-Larsen 1979

Typeset by Photo-Graphics, Honiton, Devon
Printed and bound in Great Britain by
Redwood Burn Ltd., Trowbridge & Esher

Contents

Foreword

Customer service is difficult to define. In the conventions of physical distribution customer service implies a level of performance in fulfilling orders. However, it is impossible to point to a set of activities which are uniquely identified as 'customer service'. Service becomes coextensive with the activities of the enterprise, and the performance measures are only the trace of the service performance.

When the project reported in this book was originally conceived, we had hoped that the companies involved would have available data on the service provided to their customers and that this could be related to their market performance. In almost all cases, the performance data was lacking. Where it was available, there was a confounding problem of other variables. The result was that we reoriented the study to look behind the statistical data, to examine the system by which service performance is created. Most of the data used in the study was either fragmentary or was collected specifically for the purpose of the study. The principal questions of concern became 'What happens to the order?' and 'What specific aspects of service are customers looking for?'

The answers to these questions led us in several different directions: to investigate the order-fulfilment process, to measure perceptions and preferences of customers, and to measure the impact of stock-outs on the final demand and the image of the retail store. The result has been: (1) specific information about the companies themselves, which were reported to their managements; (2) insights into the process of service; and (3) development of a conceptual framework of customer service as a strategic element in interorganisational relationships.

The project was initiated at Cranfield School of Management by Professor Martin Christopher who solicited the support of the sponsoring companies. Professors Philip Schary from Oregon State University and Tage Skjott-Larsen from Copenhagen School of Business Administration joined him to carry out the investigation which extended from July 1976 to July 1977.

All of the companies involved are dealing with consumer goods. The original intent was to provide a degree of comparability. These companies turned out to be quite heterogeneous in their organisations, performance and markets. This variety turns out to be useful, however, in introducing a range of service problems for consideration. The situations which we have recorded are of organisations in transition. The technological evolution of data-processing systems alone would ensure that. However, they are also evolving in their own managerial perspectives on service itself. What was specifically observed in the course of the study will by now have changed. What is of more permanent value is the conceptual orientation of customer service and how it can be managed as an integral component of strategy.

The book owes a great deal to the sponsoring companies and the managers who gave us their time and insights.

The book also developed as a result of collegial review. While none have seen the entire effort, individually they have made valuable comments on specific parts of the manuscript. They include Professors John Bigelow, Boris W. Becker and Barry Shane of Oregon State University, and Frederick Beier of the University of Minnesota.

We also owe a debt of gratitude to the stalwart typists who so willingly gave their time to the production of the manuscript: Mrs Susan Ellinwood, Mrs Donna Carsner and Miss Persephone Powell. Finally, we recognise the burden that this book has placed on our long-suffering wives and families.

We can only take credit for our errors of commission and omission....

Corvallis, Oregon
Cranfield, England,
Copenhagen, Denmark

1 The concept of customer service

The concept

Customer service is like the end of a pipeline. The pipeline is the flow of goods from a supplier to a customer. This flow is managed through a set of activities identified as physical distribution. To develop this analogy, customer service performs a matching function, linking the pipeline of the supplier with that of the customer and the terms under which this matching takes place are then the issues of customer service. Directing and controlling this matching process becomes a means of influencing the relationships between buyer and seller: a customer service strategy.

In business practice, customer service has been long in evidence. However, it achieved formal recognition only with the development of the physical distribution concept. Physical distribution itself, a conceptualisation of the movement of goods not as a set of piecemeal activities but as an integrated system, also has historical roots [2]. It has only been within the last quarter-century that the field of physical distribution itself has gained formal recognition. This has been a result of several factors: awareness of the costs of distribution, the increased options in distribution technology and the rise of the computer and its ability to handle large quantities of information, thus enabling distribution activities to be managed as a system.

Early definitions of physical distribution did not specifically include the concept of customer service. Wendall Stewart [4] is generally credited with one of the earliest statements of recognition of the role of customer service within the physical distribution concept. The acceptance and expansion of customer service as a concept on its own, however, has taken hold rapidly. The profession of physical distribution management has shown increasing awareness and adoption of service as a tenet of physical distribution, manifested in the development of practices and organisational structures to deal specifically with this area.

Customer service has become important for three reasons: first is the concept of system integration. The essence of physical distribution is that functional activities involved in the movement of goods to market are interrelated and that decisions in any one area may have significant impacts in other areas as well. This also extends to relationships between firms where actions taken within the functional areas of a supplier may affect the performance and decisions of a customer. The system relationship makes the decisions by a supplier significant to customers, both in planning their internal activities and in the customers' evaluations of potential suppliers.

A second force encouraging emphasis on service has been a trend towards intensification of competition. The emergence of oligopolistic market structures in worldwide product markets encourages high levels of competitive interdependence. These rivalries intensify as demand softens, leading to price and service competition to maintain shares of the market.

A third reason is the recognition of the costs of distribution as one of the last frontiers of management efficiency. Service to customers involves a trade-off between the cost of service and the service that customer receives. The level of service must therefore be specified if costs are going to be controlled.

Analysis of the physical distribution system has itself evolved through several distinct stages of development. As recognition increased that distribution activities spanned the organisation, the logical extension was to aggregate these into a total cost of distribution. This implied that all of these areas were interrelated and therefore should be managed as an integral system. From this came the concept of the 'system trade-off', the idea that changes in outlay or performance characteristics in one area of the firm would directly affect performance and costs in another. Each activity should then be considered for its effect on the entire system. Management of physical distribution involved a system of exchanges within the organisation to achieve a total optimisation rather than a suboptimisation by functional areas. Physical distribution was cost-oriented.

When Stewart asked the question 'How can physical distribution generate sales?' [4, p.67], the concept was then extended to less tangible areas, which to some degree come in conflict with the total-cost approach. Service is presumed to increase sales, but it also increases the costs of doing business. Increasing the availability of products through higher inventory service levels may increase sales through fewer stock-outs and greater dependence by customers on suppliers' inventories, but it also increased the investment in finished goods inventory. Management should then be concerned as to whether the level of service is high, while at the same time they should be concerned about their efficiency in providing this service.

Customer service is thus responsible for enlarging the concept of physical distribution from a total-cost orientation to a total-system orientation. This then raises the question: 'What is being balanced against costs?' The answer from theory would be the revenues generated by increments of service. Total systems optimisation is then a profit-maximising behaviour. This assumes that the revenues resulting from improved customer service can be determined. In most cases this is difficult, if not impossible. How then can we deal with service operationally as part of the physical distribution concept? Service is a market-determined variable; it is thus an ultimate constraint on the system operation. Therefore service has become a minimal performance constraint, against which the total costs should then be minimised.

The meaning of customer service

There is no generally accepted definition of customer service. The concept is often defined by describing the activities which are considered most important in the interfaces between a company and its customers. Therefore the definitions tend to be highly situational. Even within a specific company the perceptions of customer service can vary from one person to another. Customer service will here be defined as *'a system organised to provide a continuing link between the time that the order is placed and the goods are received with the objective of satisfying customer needs on a long-term basis'*. The analogy to this definition is *'service from a pipeline'*.

This definition is general in scope and emphasises the long-term relationships between supplier and customer.

The elements of customer service can be categorised in various ways. LaLonde and Zinszer [3] made a distinction between three groups of customer service elements:

1   pre-transaction elements
2   transaction elements
3   post-transaction elements.

The *pre-transaction elements* of customer service relate to corporate policies or programmes, e.g. written statements of service policy, adequacy of organisational structure and system flexibility.

The *transaction elements* are those customer service variables directly involved in performing the physical distribution function. The most commonly quoted elements within this group are:

1   product availability
2   order cycle time — average and consistency
3   order status information
4   order preparation
5   order size and order frequency.

The *post-transaction elements* of customer service are generally supportive of the product while in use. For instance, product warranty, parts and repair service, procedures for customer complaints, and product replacements.

Activities employed in customer service

Customer service performance is the net result of the efforts in various activity centres in the firm. Normally, the following activities are employed in creating customer service levels:
1 inventory
2 transportation
3 warehousing
4 order transmission and processing
5 forecasting
6 production planning and control.

Inventory determines the ultimate performance of the system by ensuring product availability at the time that the customer places his order.

Transportation provides customer service elements such as delivery time, delivery-time consistency, damage control, packaging and materials-handling requirements, ease of returns, ability to handle expedited shipments and trans-shipments through more than a single carrier.

Warehousing influences customer service in terms of order-filling time, accuracy, condition of goods in storage, materials-handling compatibility with the customer's system and the degree of unitisation required.

Order transmission and processing determines both the degree of difficulty experienced by the customer in placing an order, and the processing-time consistency provided by the supplier.

Forecasting serves to anticipate customer needs so that inventory and production decisions can be taken in time to meet demand.

Production planning and control influences product availability in finished goods inventory or shipment dates to the customer through setting production schedules.

All of these activities are important in establishing a desired level of customer service performance. They are also all inter-dependent; if one activity fails, the system fails, creating poor performance, and unstabilising workloads in other areas, resulting in the end in poor cost-effectiveness for the system as a whole. A failure in sales forecasting then may influence production planning which then results in low product availability in finished goods inventory. This in turn may either result in lost sales or an increased number of back orders which may in turn delay order processing and hence extend the order cycle time. This may result in the need to expedite shipments which increases the cost of service to the customer.

None of these elements can thus be considered independently of one another. Management of customer service and even more important the development of customer service strategy must deal with the problem as an integrated system. Decisions to change one element must take into account the system impacts.

Approaches to strategy

The traditional approach to customer service has been supplier-oriented. In the absence of concerted effort to establish what the customer desires, management has typically made its own judgements, established standards and measured performance. These decisions may not be completely without customer inputs, but seldom do suppliers make formal surveys of customers to establish more precisely the nature of market preferences. More recently, some suppliers have reported efforts to obtain customer indications at least of their relative satisfaction with the service that they are receiving. A few formal studies have been reported in the literature, but these do not appear to be widespread in application.

Service is a relative concept within an industry. What is regarded as a high level of service in one industry may not be impressive in another. Much depends on market structure, the nature of the product and the present level of competitive activity.

Service strategy under these conditions is often considered to be to maintain a competitive parity, responding to the perceived level of competitors' service. Typical service objectives stated by distribution executives are to offer service levels which match, but do not necessarily exceed those of competition.

Within an industry, there may be a differentiation among classes of customers, with different combinations of service variables. These are then frequently equated against price levels. Low service distribution to small grocery outlets may be deliberately planned in order to keep prices low, creating costs for the customer which he absorbs himself. This can be compared with the levels of service offered to major chains which absorb customer costs which they would otherwise have to bear. In both these cases, there is an added dimension of order size which also affects prices and costs, so that direct price-service comparisons should take volume into account as well.

Service as a competitive weapon is also vulnerable to imitation. Any competitive advantages gained through service without major system alterations can become shortlived. Under conditions of intensive rivalry, service can be subject to almost immediate imitation. Therefore, short-run strategies to gain a competitive advantage through aggressive service may prove to be shortlived and costly failures.

Service is often considered in too narrow a perspective. The service provided by a manufacturer to his customer is only one link in an extended chain of buying and selling arrangements identified as a marketing channel: a cooperating system of middlemen with a dominating interest in earning profits through movement of the product to the final consumer. The problem in service is that, if these middlemen are independent of each other, the service provided by one supplier to his customer may have no measurable effect either on channel costs as a whole or on the ability of the final reseller to meet the requests of his customer. What may happen is that channel members may actually work at cross-purposes, such as the example of a manufacturer who increased service to dealers but found that the dealers were then reducing their own inventories in response; the final customer experienced no difference in the service provided. The problem is that service is often considered to be a series of almost completely separate events without any effort to relate it to a broader context.

This broader context provides customer service with a different perspective. The purpose of customer service is to create larger systems out of smaller components. Service must meet the needs of both customer and supplier. This requires a matching of system characteristics between buyer and seller. Carried to a logical conclusion, customer service becomes coextensive with the marketing channel spanning, through a series of interfaces, the raw-material supplier and the final reseller.

The physical distribution concept strictly speaking deals with problems of suboptimisation within the firm. Channel management on the other hand involves the organisation of independent firms into an integrated system. The physical distribution task in a channel context then requires recognition of this extended interrelationship so that physical goods movement activities of all channel members are coordinated. The objectives are management of channel performance and resources to achieve acceptable performance at the final point of sale at the lowest possible system costs.

Customer service then takes on a strategic orientation in two areas: one is concerned with strategy and the individual firm. Here service becomes part of a broader marketing strategy designed to strengthen the objectives of a single channel member. The other is involved in the establishment and management of a channel system where channel objectives dominate over those of any one firm, and the channel itself becomes organised to achieve system profits which are then divided as rewards for individual channel members.

The approach in this book is to begin with the individual firm and a conventional perspective on customer service. This pespective then becomes a basis for later expansion as management horizons shift from the firm to the channel and from the short- to the long-run, in which the system is open for substantive change in organisation and management.

The book

The purpose of this book is to probe broadly into the meaning of customer service. The starting point was a number of company studies where the initial task was simply to audit the customer service operations of those companies, summarise their activities, and describe the extent and the reactions of customers to the present level of service. However as the study progressed, it became apparent to us that customer service was being more broadly construed and practised than is indicated by the current literature in the area. Two generalisations emerged: that customer service, instead of being the province of physical distribution alone, was also a concern of marketing and production and that service relationships will change over time. Effective management of the service function thus requires a sense of strategy, to determine what this relationship with customers should be in the future. None of the individuals in the companies involved openly expressed this view, but it became clear that this broader perspective was important to the review of the customer service problem.

The research was originally planned as a customer service audit. The concept of an audit in physical distribution is relatively new. An audit, according to Christopher, Walters and Gattorna [1, p. 49], is 'the appraisal of the existing situation or position, both in terms of the external environment and the internal operating environment of the company'. It operates at two levels: at a micro-level where it is concerned with present operations and resources of the firm, and at a macro-level where it is involved in assessing the environmental impact on the organisation. A customer service audit according to these authors would then be concerned with:

1   product availability

2   delivery time
3   delivery reliability
4   order processing and progressing
5   picking errors
6   back-order procedures
7   returned goods.

Performance along these dimensions would then be compared to market performance to establish statistical relationships which then would lend themselves to analysis.

A number of companies were solicited for possible participation in the project; these were reduced to seven by self-selection and included six consumer-goods manufacturers and one major food retailer. The recruitment of consumer-goods companies was deliberate in order to provide a common basis of comparison. All these companies sold their products through retailers and in some cases wholesalers. Much of the variation which was anticipated in industrial marketing could thus be avoided in dealing with a more homogeneous market.

Each of these manufacturing companies agreed to the concept of the audit. The retailer participated with specific interest in studying the behaviour of consumers as they encountered stock-outs in the store. In that sense, their portion of the project stands alone.

The audit procedure involved extensive interviews with each company, examining every aspect of the order-processing system, discussion with operating managers involved even indirectly in customer order fulfilment, including sales, production and systems managers. In addition, extensive contact was made with customers to establish the perceived quality of customer service. In some cases this was done through informal interviews; in others it led to formal research programmes.

The original objective of part of the audit, the collection of performance data, could not be achieved in more than a partial way. Data was either not complete or did not measure a sufficient number of dimensions to describe system performance. The design of the approach to the problem then shifted to a more qualitative, more intensive investigation of

individual systems. The results of this research are the subject
of this book.

The book can be divided into nine parts. Chapter 2
summarises the current discussion about customer service, to
establish the level of current understanding of the field.
Chapter 3 describes the operations practices of the six
companies in providing service to customers, dealing with
performance, management and process organisation. Chapter
4 presents the results of specific formal research into customer
perceptions and preferences in customer service. Chapter 5
extends the concept of customer service to the consumer
through the study of consumer response to out-of-stock
situation in the supermarket. In Chapter 6, the concept of
customer service as a process is explored, introducing the
concept of organising the processing system as a
communications network. In Chapter 7, the issues of customer
service strategy are developed, dealing with both short- and
long-term decision horizons. This will be matched in Chapter 8
by discussion of the problems of control over customer service
strategies. Chapter 9 deals with research methodology in
identifying customer perceptions. Chapter 10 summarises the
current state of customer service and indicates directions for
future research.

Conclusion

Customer service is an old concept, but it has received a new
emphasis with the rising importance of physical distribution
and awareness that the terms of service can influence demand.
Customer service has taken on a narrow focus, defined by the
characteristics of order fulfilment and delivery. There are,
however, other aspects which give it a strategic importance
extending beyond its normally accepted role.

The purpose of this book then is to consider an expanded
view of service, starting with the conventional definition but
moving beyond to look at service in a strategic setting, and

examining long-term relationships between suppliers and customers.

References

1. Christopher, Martin, David Walters and John Gattorna, *Distribution Planning and Control* (Farnborough, England: Gower Press, 1977).
2. Depuit, Jules. 'On the Measurement of the Utility of Public Works.' reprinted in *International Economics Papers No. 2* (translated from the French by R.H. Barback (London: Macmillan and Company, Ltd, 1952), p. 100, cited in James L. Heskett, Nicholas A. Glaskowsky, Jr and Robert M. Ivie, *Business Logistics,* 2nd edition (New York: Ronald Press Company, 1973), p. 29.
3. LaLonde, B.J. and Paul H. Zinszer. Customer Service: *Meaning and Measurement* (Chicago: National Council of Physical Distribution Management, 1976).
4. Stewart, Wendall, M. 'Physical Distribution: Key to Improved Volume and Profits,' *Journal of Marketing,* Vol.29 (January 1965), pp.65-70.

2 The corporate context of customer service

Customer service has been a neglected element in corporate strategy. In the previous chapter, the concept of customer service was reviewed and placed into a setting of inter-organisational relationships. In this chapter, we will focus on the role of customer service within the specific context of the manufacturing organisation, in order to establish an organisational perspective and also to identify the essential elements which create service.

The essential definition of customer service

The traditional view of physical distribution stresses the systemic nature of the process. Functional areas are related by their contribution to the flow of goods to market. The principal focus has been on the management of the resource *inputs* to the system, i.e. controlling the costs of each functional area such as inventory and transportation, in order to minimise the total cost of distribution. This leads to cost exchanges among these functional areas, known as the system trade-off. The emphasis on cost has tended to exclude consideration of the functional objective of the system, the *outputs* that the system creates. These are not only the product flows themselves, but also the terms under which this flow is provided. These terms, the conditions of response to orders, are generally known as service. This side appears to be relatively neglected in the push to minimise system costs. Service to customers only becomes important as business firms recognise its impact in the market place.

The underlying purpose of any distribution system is to produce *product availability* — 'having the right product in the right place at the right time'. Determining the specific nature of these conditions and matching the performance of the system to these requirements is what customer service is all about. Customer service plays an unrecognised role in serving the market place. Marketing strategies presume that products will be delivered in accordance with the expectations of customers. Service is the precondition on which other strategies must be based.

The concept of product availability however must be interpreted in broad conceptual terms. When we consider retail mail order or custom production orders, availability fails to define the service necessary to meet market requirements. The 'right place at the right time' is then a process of meeting the customer's prior expectations. A customer who places an order with an understanding that the product will not be delivered for six weeks has fixed in his mind a set of expectations. Service becomes acceptable so long as these terms are met and there are no better alternatives that are called to his attention. Service fails when performance lags behind expectation. It also fails when it does not match the performance of competition.

The concept of availability must then be redefined in larger terms, to include the capacity to serve as well as the product on the shelf. Finished goods inventory on hand can be construed in this capacity perspective as the ability to serve the immediate needs of the customer. A production schedule open to new orders can also be construed as presenting availability, when an acceptable order lead time can be presented to a customer. The essential element in the terms availability or capacity is then to match the customer's expectations so that he can meet his own needs or that of his customer under the best of possible alternative conditions.

The time-effects of customer service

Whether we are measuring availability or capacity, the event of service creates both short- and long-term effects. The short-term aspects of service encompass the individual successes or failures which, if carefully controlled, produce little effect in the long-run. The cumulative effect of short-term performances however have a strategic importance for the growth and survival of the organisation.

Short-run decisions about customer service are concerned with the cost of the lost sale. Service from high levels of inventory, precise delivery schedules or adequate production capacity are all short-term stratagems to avoid the penalties of failures to meet customers' expectations. Traditionally, these penalties are the loss of the immediate sale, the cost of back-ordering and special handling, or even the possible loss of future patronage of an individual's custom. These losses may be considerable, but they are not insurmountable in themselves. Their precise magnitude is however difficult to assess in advance. How much patronage will be diverted because of stock-outs is difficult to measure. Work by Walters [9] and Walter and LaLonde [8] provide some evidence through interviews with consumers about hypothetical stock-outs. Further evidence is presented in Chapter 5. Nevertheless, the problem eludes precise quantification.

The long-term effects have more potency, but are even more difficult to assess. Part of the problem is that customer service involves system relationships between customers and sellers extending over considerable periods of time. Only repeated performance determines the actual level of service provided, and this must be measured through controlled statistical indicators. If performance fails to meet buyers' expectations, or if it fails to respond to changes in these expectations, customers presumably turn to other suppliers. Market shares and sales decline. Service is then responsible for the maintenance or diversion of a stream of potential revenues and profits extending over undetermined future time-intervals.

Those long-term relationships imply then that because of these effects customer service expenditures are an investment in maintaining market positions. The returns cannot be precisely estimated, first because the precise behaviour of customers and competitors cannot be predicted, and second because the only directly measurable results are those of failure. Positive service does not bring with it directly positive rewards; these are generally attributed to sales and market development efforts.

Consideration of customer service as a specific category of investment is virtually unknown in modern corporate circles. Service expenditures are absorbed into a widely diversified set of departmental budgets. Their combined impacts then are seldom considered as a single unit, either as a competitive weapon in the marketing arsenal or as a collection of costs which can be related to a specific decision.

Identifiable or not, service does have an impact on the organisation. Higher levels of inventory service require investment in stocks to be placed in convenient locations. Precise delivery requires management and investment in transport capacity to ensure the absorption of normal fluctuations in demand. Production process capacity must be available to meet the needs of incoming orders. These policy decisions, however, often are made in widely scattered functional areas and thus are not linked in organisationally coherent patterns. The result is the absence of central guidance for service decisions and consequently a set of piecemeal choices which fail to consider overall effects on either costs or markets.

This phenomenon has begun to gain some recognition, in both shifts of functional activities and establishment of a locus of control. The location of activities such as order processing within distribution recognises the relationship of that activity to distribution performance. The movement of production scheduling in some firms to marketing and distribution is a response to a similar problem. The emergence of direct managerial authority for customer service itself, however, lags behind, as we shall note in the discussion ahead. Nevertheless there is an awakening to the need for customer service management if service is to achieve more effectiveness.

The organisational need is to integrate functions to utilise resources which are already being committed, to match outlays to the service provided. Only at this point can we fruitfully discuss the concept of a strategy for customer service.

Strategic implications

Customer service implies a strategy, whether that strategy is recognised by the organisation or not. What then should be the measurable objective of a service strategy? Market performance is traditionally measured by sales volume, market share and profitability. Customer service has a role to maintain markets rather than to initiate them. These traditional criteria are then asymmetric. Success is keeping the status quo; failures result in market losses, as customers turn towards alternative suppliers. The difficulties in establishing global measures then leave service as a strategy without a specific goal other than to operate without market changes.

A significant aspect of customer service is that it becomes remote from the final market. Even in consumer goods industries, seldom are consumers directly involved except through their purchase behaviour. The phenomenon of brand loyalty is based on the purchase habits of individual consumers, measured through data on repeat purchases over time. The actual choice of products from which the consumer can choose however has been predetermined by some intermediate buyer. Product availability is one criterion among several which influence buyers for retail organisations in making their selections. This has caused such writers as Farley to note [2] that brand loyalty itself is based on the selection which the buyer has already made for the consumer rather than the free expression of consumer preferences. Product availability is thus potentially a highly influential factor in determining final market success. This influence is however seldom recognised.

How important is customer service? More specifically, how do buyers compare the importance of service to other marketing decision variables offered by the supplier? Perrault and Russ [5] surveyed industrial purchasing officers using examples of standardised products and found that distribution service was considered second in importance only to product quality as a deciding criterion for vendor selection. Moreover, more than one-third of these purchasing officers indicated that they would cancel the order if it were not available for shipment when ordered.

These findings were further reinforced in a study by Cunningham and Roberts [1]. This investigation of the valve and pump manufacturing industry evaluated the service provided by suppliers of steel castings and forgings. Delivery reliability emerged as the primary element influencing the choice of supplier, even more important than technical advice.

Both of these surveys dealt with products which are highly similar, where product differentiation is less important than it might be in markets with higher levels of technological development. Nevertheless, the surveys describe conditions common to many markets and industries.

In contrast to this is a study of supplying manufacturers, sponsored by the National Council of Physical Distribution Management in the United States, by LaLonde and Zinszer [4]. Their findings indicated that among the manufacturing companies surveyed, customer service was ranked third in importance, behind the marketing elements of product and price. Evidence such as this, however, can be evaluated in either of two ways. First, it could indicate a low appraisal of the value of service as a competitive weapon. Alternatively, it could indicate that service is uniformly high and therefore offers no further competitive advantage. The first is supported by their data which shows that only 31 per cent of the firms surveyed had actually instituted formal policies on customer service. This suggests a low management priority.

Buyers apparently take the quality of service much more seriously than do manufacturers. These studies dealt with different markets and thus may not be directly comparable.

Nevertheless there is a strong intimation of neglect, that service has been underemphasised as a strategic weapon in the struggle to attain and maintain market position.

Cost-benefit analysis of customer service

Customer service as a system produces results which are not easily recognised. Clearly they are only indirectly related to the revenues which service is presumed to protect. The traditional business yardsticks, the profit and loss statement and comparisons of incremental revenues and costs cannot be applied without considerable adaptation.

One approach to the evaluation of service has been to establish the cost of a stock-out, which is then the value in effect of single failure of the system. The frequency with which it occurs would then provide an indication of system performance. This, however, measures only the extreme case. Distribution performance is not normally practised as 'brinkmanship' but involves more subtlety, producing equally subtle reaction among customers. This is described by Stephenson and Willett [7], hypothesising the response by customers to service variables:

> 'Variation in shipment time directly affects the consignee's investment in inventory, buying and inventory carrying costs and the frequency of stock-outs producing non-recoupable lost sales. Sensitivity to his own profits will prompt the consignee to favour suppliers who provide for consistent service. Erratic delivery schedules, on the other hand, can negatively affect the supplier's sales by prompting the consignee to direct orders to alternative sources. At best, the supplier may be faced with high compensating costs to maintain a customer that is receiving deficient service.'

Relatively few studies have been made of the retail buyer and his actual perception of distribution service performance.

Another study by Willett and Stephenson [11] examined the perception of retail druggists concerning delivery lead-time and their ability to discern differences in supplier performance. They noted that 'buyers could discriminate among even small differences in physical distribution service times and their ratings of satisfaction with service were a linear function of service time'. This study, however, examined only the *perceptions* of retail buyers and did not examine their response in terms of actual behaviour in vendor selection.

An article by Hutchinson and Stolle [3] demonstrating the use of survey research in customer service alluded to a study which measured response among retailers to differing levels of customer service. They commented:

> [While] the *sales effects* of different levels of service can be determined with successful accuracy. Their measurement does present more difficulty because they are less visible... As for the effects of providing really good service, these are usually more difficult to measure precisely because the results are often clouded by other marketing actions of the company and of competitors.

A more recent paper by Shycon and Sprague [6] investigated buyer reactions to service in the food distribution industry. A model was developed to establish a cost of failure to maintain adequate service by suppliers to major food chains. They found that buyers after some experience with poor service were sufficiently provoked to remove products from the stores' order lists, reduce shelf space allocations, and even to refuse to list new products that the supplier wished to introduce. In effect the buyer was actually punishing the supplier for poor service.

These studies indicate a mixture of both long- and short-term effects: presumably higher level of expenditure on service will bring long-term results in greater customer acceptance, larger market shares, and general benefits to marketing strategy, some of which are not obstensibly related to distribution.

Hypothetically, market response can be converted into a market response function. The specific shape of the relationship may be conjectural, but in general it describes a positive relationship between service outlays and sales as shown in Figure 2.1. Up to a point, higher levels of service outlays result in increasing returns. At some point, however, these returns will diminish. In contraposition to the market response curve is a cost function which shows exponentially increasing costs as service provided increases. At some point (L) the sum of the revenues lost through service failures and the cost of providing service are minimised, indicating the expenditure level which would produce the highest profitability. The diagram thus suggests an optimal level for service.

The response and cost functions describe a system trade-off between cost and service. The central task of customer service management is to achieve and maintain a balance between the benefits to customers from service and the related costs. The concrete problem is that costs are incurred in real terms, and response to service is measured if not as abstract measures, at least in ways that are intermixed with other marketing actions.

Establishing a cost for the service package appears to be straightforward. Walters for example [9] provides a systematic approach to deriving the total cost of a stock-out, involving the consumer, the retailer and the manufacturer.

As mentioned before, Walters' approach confronts only the cost of a single crisis event. It does not deal with the concept of a continuum of adjustment, implied by Willett and Stephenson earlier in our discussion.

A similar approach was offered by Weeks [10]. The approach is similar to Walters' in that he attempts to identify the cost elements in the stock-out. He has also incorporated a concept of goodwill which presumably can be capitalised in terms of future patronage, in addition to the costs of back-ordering and related expense (see Figure 2.3).

Logistics is consistently involved in trade-offs: between costs of different functional areas, between costs and service, and even between types of service. These may be differentiated at three levels. In the final consumer market, the exchange is

Figure 2.1 The cost benefit of customer service

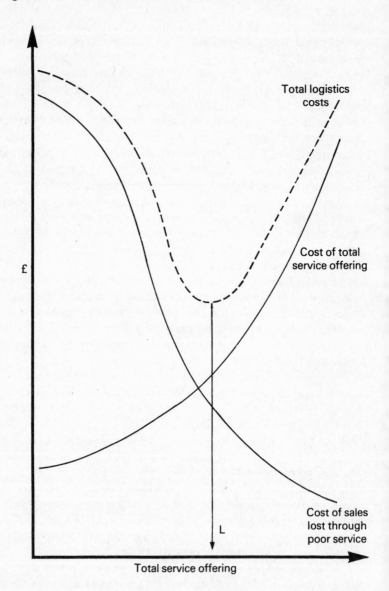

Figure 2.2 Stock-out process: basic model

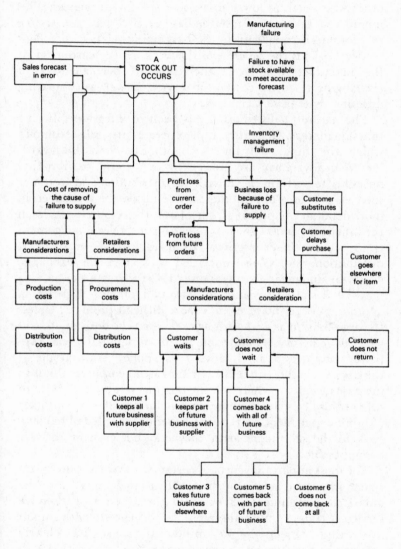

Source: Walters, D.W. [9]

between market share and product availability. If availability is low, however, perhaps this might be compensated for in other ways, such as lower prices and special allowances. This might also be true at intermediate levels. Here the service relationship is caught up in the bargaining relationship. Poor service weakens the seller's position *vis-à-vis* the customer. At the manufacturer's level, the trade-off becomes one of exchanging resources (costs) for service, as well as comparing differing types of service.

The nature of distribution has been to integrate differing functional areas. Generally, it involves a matrix relationship in which the functional lines of authority flow downward, hierarchically. They are crossed by the lateral coordination necessary to perform the 'mission' of distribution and customer service. This idea of customer service missions is developed in more detail in Chapter 10. Control over the resources resides in the functional areas. The task of customer service management is to secure these resources from each area in turn. If distribution were solely concerned with costs, the exchange would be much easier to visualise: a cost increase in one area may be desirable because it permits a greater decrease in another. Service, however, is a more difficult problem. Unless the organisation as a whole is agreed about the desirability and general goals of service, each of the functional areas may present obstacles to an effective service policy. For example, if the stock controller argues for an increase in corporate funds to increase inventory, where will the tangible results come from to support his decision? Increases in revenue are the responsibility of other departments so that the benefits not only fail to come back to the sacrificing area, they may not even be directly demonstrable.

The most important aspect of customer service is its long-run system impact. It is also the most difficult to demonstrate. The only strong arguments come from the absence of effective service. Strategy must therefore be developed with broad overriding objectives in mind. It must be clearly communicated through the entire corporate organisation with

Figure 2.3 The Cost of a Stock-out

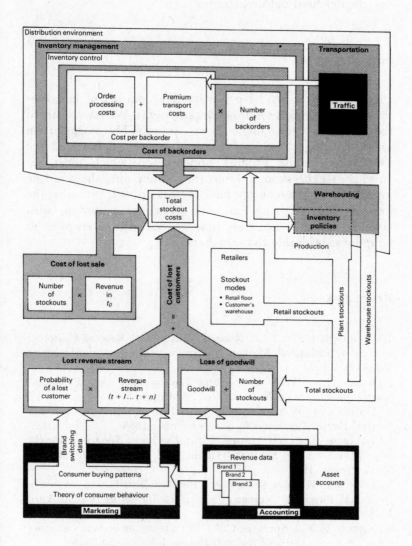

Source: Unpublished Master's Paper of J. Duane Weeks, *The Effect of Inventory Control and Stock-out Costs on the Management of a Multi-Echelon Distribution System* (University Park: Pennsylvania State University, 1974)

adequate measures of functional performance. Otherwise it may be defeated before it begins.

Summary

In this chapter, we have presented a concept of customer service embracing a system of organisations. We have restored the focus to the single firm, presumably engaged in manufacturing. Customer service has been defined as the availability of the product under terms which meet the customer's expectations. From that standpoint, the strategic implications of the concept have been examined, exploring the impact of considering customer service as a system, with benefits and costs. The costs, however, may ultimately prove to be more measurable than the benefits.

References

1. Cunningham, M.T. & Roberts, D.A., 'The Role of Customer Service in Industrial Marketing' *European Journal of Marketing* Vol.8 No.1 1974
2. Farley, J.U. 'Why does Brand Loyalty vary over Products?' *Journal of Marketing Research* Vol.1 1 August 1964
3. Hutchinson, W.M. & Stolle, J.F., 'How to Manage Customer Service' *Harvard Business Review* November 1968
4. LaLonde, B.J. and Zinszer, P.A., *Customer Service: Meaning and Measurement* National Council of Physical Distribution Management, 1976
5. Perreault, W.D. & Russ, F.A., 'Physical Distribution Service in Industrial Purchase Decisions' *Journal of Marketing* Vol.40 April 1976
6. Shycon, H.N. & Sprague, C.R., 'Put a price tag on your customer servicing levels' *Harvard Business Review* July/August 1975
7. Stephenson, P.R. & Willett, R.P., 'Consistency: The Carriers' Ace in the Hole' *Transportation Journal* Vol.8 No.3 1969

8. Walter, C.K. and LaLonde, B.J., 'Development and Tests of Two Stock-out Cost Models' *International Journal of Physical Distribution* Vol.5 No.3 1975

9. Walters, D.W., 'The Cost of a Stock-Out' *International Journal of Physical Distribution* Vol.5 No.1 1974

10. Weeks, J.D. 'The Effect of Inventory Control and Stock-out Costs on the Management of a Multi-Echelon Distribution System.' Unpublished Paper, Pennsylvania State University 1974

11. Willett, D.T. & Stephenson, P.R., 'Determinants of Buyer Response to Physical Distribution Service' *Journal of Marketing Research* Vol.VI August 1969

3 The process of customer service*

It has already been noted that customer service is an underemphasised area in the development of phsyical distribution service. Information comparing what individual companies are doing in this area is extremely limited.

This chapter examines the customer service practices of six consumer products companies operating in Britain. The survey was taken during the autumn of 1976 and the winter and spring of 1977. The six companies were all manufacturers of consumer products: two in food products, two in other non-food, non-durable products, and two in consumer durable goods. The complete emphasis on consumer products was chosen in order to achieve even a small measure of comparability. All these companies sell through resellers. Two were using wholesalers for a large part of their business. All of them had dealings in some degree with retailers; three of the four which did not emphasise wholesalers nevertheless did sell a share of their products through wholesalers. The common denominator was that all of them were selling to buyers for ultimate sale to the general public.

The survey consisted of intensive individual investigation of the service practices of each of these companies. The procedure of the investigation included the examination of company data on service performance where these existed,

*Earlier versions of this chapter have appeared in Robert House (editor) *Applied Distribution Research* (Columbus, Ohio: The Ohio State University, 1977) and *Organisation Marked Og Samfund,* Vol.15, No.3.

probing through interviews to identify the order fulfilment processes, and establishing the relationships of customer service and distribution in general to other parts of the organisation. The focus in this chapter is on the order-fulfilment process, the supply side of customer service. Another essential part of the customer service investigation involved investigation of customer perception of service. This will be the subject of the succeeding chapter.

The discussion will proceed from a preliminary discussion of the customer service environment to comparison of (a) service performance among the six companies, (b) management of the order-fulfilment process, and (c) organisation of the process itself.

The environment of customer service

Environmental factors appear to be influential in determining the state of customer service. Practices which are commonplace in one country may be difficult to pursue in another, even with managements of relatively equal sophistication. There are several environmental factors which have affected the orientation towards customer service:

1 the geography of Britain
2 government transportation policy
3 channels of distribution
4 adoption of new technology
5 the state of the economy
6 the management acceptance of the physical distribution concept
7 management attitudes towards customer service

Geographic influences tend to favour the development of uniform levels of customer service in Britain. The market is compact and densely populated. With the exception of London, it is dispersed over the landscape with relative evenness, in contrast to much of the United States, for example. The country is well connected by an extensive road network which enables delivery to any major population centres within two days' journey time.

The improvements in the road network brought on by the extension of the motorway network have reduced the need for branch warehouses. The tendency has been to centralise distribution into limited numbers of distribution centres unless there are an extremely large number of drop points. The one exception in the study maintained 32 depots serving 46 000 drop points.

Transportation practices tend to favour private carriage. Only two of the six companies relied heavily on for-hire transport. Almost all goods are carried by truck, eliminating a major customer service decision whether to accumulate orders into sufficiently large quantities to ship by rail. Private transport is encouraged by the Transportation Act of 1968 which encourages private carriers to offer their services to other shippers as well.

Improvements in transportation have reduced the need for intermediate middlemen such as wholesalers. The result has been a trend towards direct channels from manufacturer to retailer. This has also meant direct delivery whenever shipment sizes warrant, while wholesalers are used only to serve smaller accounts. The food retailing industry maintains networks of warehouses to receive and distribute products from manufacturers, but retailers also encourage direct delivery to stores on many product categories. Among non-food companies, the non-durables companies relied on wholesalers. The durables companies delivered direct to stores.

This direct relationship between manufacturer and retailer, particularly in food distribution, has enabled a high degree of innovation to take place. One outstanding example has been the introduction and adoption of the cage pallet, a large merchandise display unit, with merchandise price-marked and loaded either at the end of the production line or in the supplier's depot, and then moved directly onto the floor of the retail store, ready for sale. In another area of innovation, common article coding and computer-linked ordering systems, there appear to be considerable delays. Individual retail chains have developed their coding systems for stock-keeping, but the need for a European as opposed to a uniquely British system has delayed development and implementation of an industry-wide code.

Order-processing appears to rely less heavily on telecommunications than, for example, is true in the United States. This appears to be determined by Post Office policies on telephone services and pricing. On the other hand, the Post Office leases dedicated lines for remote computer operation and the cost is lower than elsewhere in Europe.

The state of the economy becomes an important factor in determining customer service policies. Service is affected by (a) aggregate demand, (b) financial policy which in the past has made inventory holding into a high-cost decision in terms of cash costs, and (c) by uncertainty about future markets, holding back potential investment in production and distribution facilities. Companies have reacted by desiring to hold less stock, particularly in higher-priced goods and luxury products, a decision which has proved sometimes to be in error as demand for these products has exceeded forecasts.

Acceptance of the physical distribution concept also has a bearing on customer service performance. The domain of the distribution manager has traditionally been that of a fleet manager for delivery vehicles. A survey made in 1974 indicated that responsibility was placed in the distribution area for inventory control for only 54 per cent and for production scheduling only 6 per cent of the responding companies.

Management attitudes towards customer service are the most difficult to measure. There is an axiom never to offer more service than absolutely necessary and not more than the competition. The historical levels of service that might be used for determining an appropriate reference point appear to have been low. The distribution director of one firm with an American subsidiary commented that the frequency of both sales calls and delivery in the American company was two to three times higher than their own practice in Britain. Customer service levels thus appear to be determined as much by historical accident as a lack of vigorous competition than by deliberate management decision.

Performance of Customer Service

Product Availability

Product availability is unquestionably the most important dimension of customer service. Surprisingly, this is also frequently outside the control of distribution but is the responsibility of production or jointly of marketing and production. A comparison of product availability for the six companies is shown in Table 3.1. For each of these firms, the formal standards, actual performance and the nature of managerial control are identified. Formal standards were established for only three of the companies in the survey. One used an ABC inventory classification system, setting target stock coverage on the basis of comparative turnover. Paradoxically, but not atypically, these objectives were only achieved for the C group; both A and B categories were below the standard. C items are slow-moving, with low risk of stock-out because of the heavy investment in cycle stock. A and B items by contrast are fast-moving items where cycle stock investment relative to turnover tends to be lower. While safety stock policies were set to protect these items against stock-out, changes in both demand and/or the rate of production tended to create frequent out-of-stock situations.

For the other two companies, the target standards were more general, based on overall measures of product turnover. High turnover items were either supplied direct from the production line or through depot stocks.

Actual stock availability performance was a major problem for five of the six companies. Several factors appeared to be involved:

1   inadequate sales forecasting
2   faulty sales allocation systems
3   long product lead time
4   limited production capacity
5   limited ability of production to respond to changes in demand
6   inadequate inventory control systems

Table 3.1 Comparison of product availability: standards, performance and control systems

Company	Standards	Actual performance	Control systems
A	ABC-classification according to volume of turnover A: 98% B: 95% C: 92%	Product availability lower than targets for A and B items A: 85% B: 85% C: 92%	Records of the stock availability for each item
B	No standards defined	Stock availability about 90%. At times, severe problems in some product lines	Recently initiated measurements of stock availability
C	Minimum inventory level of two days' stock on hand	Stock-outs not considered as a problem. Outstanding orders can often be filled overnight from production	No measurements of stock availability
D	No standards defined	Highly seasonal. Usually high product availability in the first half of the year and low towards the end of the year Product availability is a severe problem	No measurements of stock availability
E	95% product availability	Severe problems in some product lines	Close control of the service level, by case and by product line. Weekly reports of shortages by depot, by product and by reasons
F	No standards defined	Poor product availability	No measurements of stock availability

Several of the firms had difficulties in forecasting future demand. In two companies this was aggravated because of highly seasonal demand characteristics and long production lead times. For one company, poor stock performance was a result of a lack of production capacity over a four-year period. Sales allocation systems are also a recurring cause of stock-outs. The purpose of the allocation system is to indicate to sales the amount of stock that each customer can order. However, if they are inaccurate or poorly administered, they may even exacerbate the problem. In one company, the allocation system had failed to close the gap between production and demand. The burden of de facto administration had fallen on the dispatch office which controlled the warehouse and delivery operations. The clerk had accumulated delivery notes, the authorisation document for shipment, and issued them on a first-in-first-out basis, in effect converting a sales priority allocation system into a delivery delay system.

The one company which did not normally experience normal inventory problems operated with short production runs and delivered to field depots overnight. However because of the breadth of their product line and their dominant share of their market, once a product becomes out-of-stock, it then creates substitute demand for other products which cannot be predicted accurately in advance.

A principal underlying cause for stock-outs is a lack of coordination among the functional areas of sales forecasting, production scheduling, inventory control and the warehouse. All of these with the exception of the warehouse are usually outside of the jurisdiction of distribution and frequently coordination may involve as many as three departments.

Only three companies used a formal reporting system to indicate performance in product availability. Only one of these systems was sufficient to ensure adequate performance. For the second, the problems of interdepartmental coordination tended to defeat the stock control system. For the third, experience had been too limited to make any statement about performance as yet. This particular company experienced severe stock-out problems in the past, holding balance orders as long as eighteen months. This is a result of an inadequate forecasting system which resulted in poor procurement policies. The planned introduction of a stock control system may reduce these problems but it will take considerable time to affect their overall performance. The other three companies had no inventory control system as such, but one was considering the introduction of a system in the future.

Order cycle time

Order cycle time along with prodcuct availability becomes a dominant element in customer service. By definition, it spans the interval between customer order placement and delivery. It can be subdivided into order acquisition and transmission, order processing and delivery. The components of specific relevance to the customer are average order cycle time and the consistency of this time. However, to understand the nature of the system it is useful to know the time interval for the component operations. These are shown in Table 3.2 as reported by these companies. Total order cycle time varied considerably from one company to another, from a minimum of from 2 to 8 days to a maximum for products in stock of 7 to 28 days. Variation in order cycle time also ranged from 2 to approximately 21 days.

Time differences within the components of order cycle time also varied substantially. Order acquisition and transmission time was constrained by the high cost of telephone communication and hence tended to rely on first-class mail service which was normally an overnight service with some variation. Delivery time is fixed by physical parameters and cannot be changed substantially. On the other hand, order processing could take as little as 1 day or as long as 2 weeks, even on orders processed only for products in stock. Within the order processing component, warehouse operations in the short run cannot be easily changed to match peak loads. The result is that the variation falls for the most part on documentation, which is then the major strategic variable in customer service time performance.

A large part of the order processing cycle is under the control of Distribution so that it is logical to expect close control over the elapsed time. In fact, all the six companies were involved with measurement of order cycle time. The degree of commitment to these measures, indicated either by the frequency of reporting or the actual performance, suggests that this control was not extensively used.

Other Service Variables

Although product availability and order cycle time appear to be the dominant dimensions, there are several other variables of importance in evaluating overall customer service performance. For these six companies, these were order status information, special orders, procedures for returns and order cancellations and minimum order size policy.

Order status information was virtually unknown among the customers of the six companies. Apart from copies of the original order and the delivery note, the customer has no other routine communication on the state of his orders. One appliance manufacturer did notify the customer prior to delivery on large orders. However, management felt that this gave the customer an opportunity to change the planned delivery date or even to cancel part of his order. Another company is planning an order acknowledgement system which would furnish hard copies of their orders in process to customers. Under certain circumstances the ability to respond to special orders may become an important customer service variable. It tends to have a symbolic rather than a functional value as most firms indicated that special order requests are relatively few. Special order procedures are seen to indicate the general level of service; the inability to meet special order requests may reflect an organisational weakness in normal service operations. Management did not express interest in special orders, considering them as a cost factor rather than a customer service benefit.

The proportion of returned and cancelled items compared to total items ordered can serve as an indicator of the efficiency

Table 3.2 Comparison of total order cycle time and methods (time measured in working days)

Code No.	Transmission	Processing	Delivery	Total order cycle	Control system
A	0-2 75% by telephone	1-5 Depending on call frequency. VDU entry on-line processing	1 Own transport	2-8	No overall control of the order cycle time. Monitoring the achievement of target delivery dates for each product ordered
B	1-2 Mostly by mail	3 Automatic typing machines	2-3 Hired transport	5-8	Total order cycle time monitored weekly by a service report recently initiated
C	1-2 Mostly by mail	1 Sense marked order forms	2-3 Own transport/ hired transport	4-6 60% within 7 working days. 96% within 9 working days	Processing time monitored by dating the documents. Transmission time closely watched. Delivery time controlled through transit advice notes returned from customers
D	2-3 99% by mail	4-23 VDU entry batch processing twice a week	1-2 Own transport/ hired transport	7-28 68% within 3 weeks. 90% within 4 weeks	Total order cycle only controlled on an ad hoc basis
E	1-2 Mostly by mail	3-5 Depending on call frequency. VDU entry batch every half hour	1 Own transport	5-7 40% of orders within 2 days. 95% within the agreed standards	Delivery times monitored on an automatic basis. Overall order cycle time checked 2-3 times a year
F	1-2 90% by mail	8-12 VDU entry batch once a day.	1 Own transport	10-15 60% within 11 days.	A customer delivery service report recently initiated. Identifies orders in excess of 21 days order cycle time.

of warehouse and delivery operations. Several companies in this project monitored this area through reporting systems capable of identifying data on sources of failure. These data included customer requests for deferred delivery, order cancellations, order duplication, overallocation of products to customers, delivery of items in error, damage and customer refusals.

A minimum order size policy is usually introduced in order to reduce costs of order processing and delivery. Several companies established minimum order policies. The company with 46000 drop units, for example, has a policy of not less than 6 cases for any one drop. Another stipulated not less than 75. Policies such as these, however, can be defeated by poor product availability, resulting in a need to hold balance orders and perform second and even third deliveries. The company with the large number of drop points would not hold balance orders if the quantity was less than six cases.

Aside from direct policy proscriptions, small orders can be discouraged in a variety of ways: reduction in sales call frequency, delaying orders until minimum quantities are achieved, and providing price incentives are a few examples. Under private carriage operations, there are difficulties in identifying the cost per drop on other than incremental or average basis, and neither appeared to affect policy in minimum order sizes.

Management of Customer Service

Successful management of customer service depends to a large extent on the presence of three conditions:
1   an organisational structure capable of achieving functional coordination under centralised control
2   an explicit customer service strategy with coherence among all the functional elements with measurable standards of performance

3 an information system for measurement and control of
   the service process to ensure that the standards established will be achieved, and that deviations will be
   recognised in time for corrective actions.

None of these stands apart. The issue of control has already
been discussed in conjunction with the performance of service.
In this section we will discuss the issues and relationship of
strategy and organisation.

Organisation

Customer service as a concept pervades the entire organisation.
Customer service involves not only direct distribution functions
such as warehouse and delivery operations but, as seen earlier,
the areas of order processing, inventory control, production
scheduling, sales forecasting and even procurement.

The central question in examining the issue of organisation
in customer service is how well the organisation is able to
coordinate the activities involved in order to achieve
centralised control. None of the companies in our study had
established a line functional position for customer service with
full responsibility for the functions that determine customer
service performance. More typical is the tendency to distribute
this responsibility among several different departments without
formal coordination or control.

Table 3.3 indicates the location of the principal activities
connected with customer service. The letters indicate the six
companies (A to F) and the position of each letter identifies the
direct line responsibility in each company.

In only two companies was there a separate department
identified for distribution, reporting to the chief executive of
the company. In three companies the Distribution manager
reports to the Production manager; in one, Distribution
reports to the Marketing director.

At a lower operating level, the problem of customer service
management is one of coordination rather than authority. The
mechanisms for achieving this appear to be informal in nature.
In the most successful company in the study, the major

organisational factor promoting effective service performance is the advance of formal organisational barriers. This is, however, dependent on the general climate and the personal skills of the individuals involved, rather than on a formal programme by senior management to manage the problem.

Table 3.3 Location of customer service functions within organisation departments

Activity	Marketing	Sales	Distribution	Production	Computer Services
Forecasting	ABCDEF				
Order processing		ACD	BE		F
Inventory control	D		BCE	AF	
Ware-housing			ABCDEF		
Dispatch			ABCDEF		

Aside from the control and coordination issues, there is another problem distinctly related to customer service: the customer's point of contact within the organisation. In general, all these companies used sales representatives for the initial point of contact. However, in most of the companies there is more than one point of contact for service matters, which can become disruptive to the organisation.

Strategy and formal policies

All of the companies held a concept of service standards, normally expressed in terms of average lead time, product availability and similar measures. For most of these firms there was, however, no conception of a total service offering, a customer service strategy.

Two exceptions were reported, representing polar extremes

in terms of strategy alternatives. One firm established standards of performance expressed in probabilistic terms such as 'delivery within 5 days with 96 per cent reliability'. These are then used in negotiation with customers as a guaranteed measure of intended performance. The service package actually includes several different elements to be specified:

1   order cycle time
2   order accuracy
3   stock levels
4   minimum order size
5   decision rules for balance orders.

This contract approach has benefits to both the supplier and the customer. First, it is an internal standard for control of distribution operation. Second, it communicates to the Sales Department the performance which Distribution can achieve in support of sales effort. Third, it communicates the level of performance to the customer as a declaration of capability, and also as a notice of the level the customer can normally expect. Higher levels of service can be negotiated specifically with the individual customer. Finally, it communicates to the rest of the buying organisation the standards to be expected, so that receiving and inventory planning activities can be incorporated around customer service performance.

In contrast, one company pursued a clear strategy to minimise customer service costs at the expense of service. Product availability was low. Orders were delayed once for batch processing twice per week on the computer and possibly again to smooth the workload in the warehouse. Delivery vans had a 95 per cent capacity utilisation rate, implying that orders could be delayed once again in order to obtain efficient routings. Service was admittedly poor, but costs were reduced drastically as a result, which was the stated management objective.

The other four firms had not, however, instituted formal service policies at the time of the study, although distribution managers used informal objectives. The question is, how far were these objectives being communicated either within their organisations or to their customers.

Customer service as a process

Customer service is an ambiguous concept. Lalonde and Zinszer [1] found that there were three relatively distinct concepts involved in the definition of customer service:

1   customer service as an acitivty
2   customer service as a set of target performance levels
3   customer service as a set of strategies, i.e. as a corporate philosophy

Depending on the choice, the evidence involved in establishing the nature of customer service would be substantially different. In the companies in the study, we were able to focus on the first two; only one company actually perceived customer service in a formalised strategic sense.

During the course of this study we found that we were actually exploring a fourth approach, necessitated by the lack of data to measure performance, and the lack of formal organisation actually committed to customer service. this was:

4   customer service as a process, involving the sequence and timing of activities involved in customer service from order placement to delivery.

Partly because of the absence of 'hard' data, and partly to better understand the underlying determinants of customer service, we examined closely the customer service process. The process involves the entire sequence of steps from the time of order placement to delivery, including both physical operations and information processing. The primary measure of process performance is order cycle time, assuming that accuracy is already ensured. The time dimension, even more than product availability, tends to fall directly within the jurisdiction of distribution management. Management of processing time provides an area for potential action even within present organisational boundaries.

Order cycle time is divisible into three component elements of which two are relatively unchanged: delivery and order transmission. The element with the greatest potential is then that part of the information system directly concerned with order processing.

Figure 3.1 Alternative configurations of the order processing system

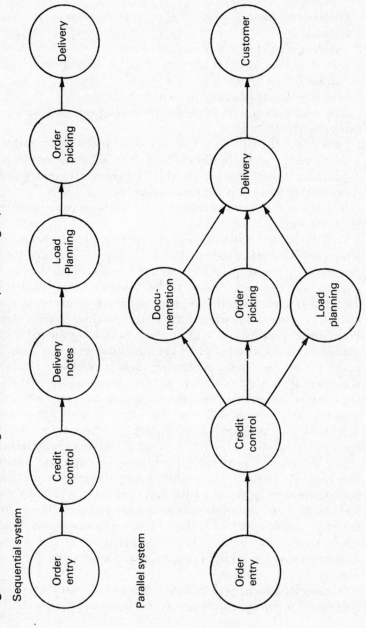

Order-processing systems design involves three types of decisions:
1   determining the system configuration
2   the degree of physical integration of processing operations on the computer
3   the scheduling of order-processing activities
The configuration of the order-processing system may take two principal forms:
1   a sequential flow where the main operations in the order-fulfilment process follow each other in a specific sequence
2   parallel flows where separable activities are performed simultaneously into parallel sequences.
The options are illustrated in Figure 3.1 with two examples from the study.

One company enters incoming orders into the computer after they have been screened and validated. They are then processed in batch, producing delivery notes which are then sent to the Dispatch Office to be assembled into delivery routes. After routing, the delivery notes are returned to the computer for compilation into order picking instructions. When order picking and loading the invoice is completed then mailed to the customer. The example shows that the flow of activities in the order-processing system follows a strict sequence with the exception of the invoicing procedure. Documents are entered into the computer at three different stages of the process with the risk of errors and omissions. There are two principal disadvantages to this system. Every operation depends on the one preceding; delays in early stages create delays in performing operations through the entire sequence. By restricting activities to single events, sequential operations take longer than parallel systems in which several operations can be undertaken simultaneously. There is, however, one distinct advantage. If uncertainty exists about stock levels, warehouse operating capacity utilisation or delivery capacity sequential processing systems require the least amount of coordination.

A parallel system was utilised by another company. This system uses a five-copy order set as the basic working document for order processing. After the order was received, the set was split into three parallel flows. The first copy was entered into the computer with order data for the customer file and updating of the inventory file. A second copy was sent to the transport planning office for load planning. The remaining three copies were then sent to the warehouse for order-picking and assembly. Following order assembly, the first copy was then returned to the computer for invoice preparation while the other two were passed to the transport office for attachment to the order itself.

This allows documentation, warehouse planning and operations, and transport planning to take place simultaneously and independently of each other. This configuration enabled the company to provide the fastest processing time that we encountered in the survey. On the other hand, the use of parallel processing required precise coordination between activity centres.

None of the companies in this study has fully integrated its order-processing system into a single computer process step to simplify document entry. Four companies were using visual display units (VDUs) which effectively integrated the functions involved in order entry. One company has investigated the integration of load planning and warehouse order selection planning into the order-processing stage on the computer. The results thus far have resulted only in computer-generated load summaries for vehicle loading.

The final element, scheduling, ultimately becomes a reflection of management policies and priorities. It begins with the timing of order entry and processing and ends with vehicle loading. Customer service is then heavily dependent on how operations are managed and the nature of utilisation of the computer.

In this study, computer order processing for all companies with one exception was done in batch. Batch processing varied from a frequency of once every half-hour to twice per week. In the first case, it is close to on-line performance. On the other, it reflected a deliberate policy to minimise computer operation costs in order to avoid conflict with other users. The net effect was to increase processing time as much as three working days. The one exception was the company in the previous example with parallel flows which operated an on-line system, but had severe difficulty in coordinating between inventory control, the warehouse and production scheduling.

The frequency of order-processing activity was only one of several sources of potential delay in the system. Others were:

1   holding completed documentation in a computer file to avoid increasing the workload in order to maintain efficient operation

2   delaying delivery of an order because of an inability to fit it into a weekly delivery route plan

3   holding an order on file to avoid creating a balance order. The order would be delivered only when the entire list of items on the order could be filled

All of these delays are clearly cost-oriented, stemming from a primary management objective to minimise costs.

The invoice is the last document to be produced in the documentation sequence. One option in designing the system is either to produce the invoice as the delivery note is prepared, or to hold it in an active file for modification after order assembly and delivery. Pre-invoicing is economical of computer file capacity and is acceptable where stock availability is high, warehouse stock positions are adequately reflected in computer stock records, few loading or delivery errors are possible and where there is little possibility of returns or refusals by customers. If these conditions are not met, then pre-invoicing may be a source of irritation to the customer and actually require substantial bookkeeping adjustments in order to verify and modify records. However, despite the fact that most of the companies involved had problems with stock availability, pre-invoicing was preferred by five of the six companies.

Implications

Examination of the internal operations of the six companies indicated a lack of management focus on the customer service problem. This suggests that coordination could be significantly improved if central management control could be established. This, however, is not likely to take place without sponsorship from the highest levels of management. Customer service involves coordination with so many functional areas inside the company that effective management does not appear possible as a lateral or cooperative control alone. The absence of a customer service strategy shifts decision making downward to lower levels in the organisation, each of which will determine their own standards with only limited coordination with other areas.

The most important variable in determining customer service performance for these six companies lies in the performance of the order-processing system. The rate of technological advance in information systems is sufficiently high to require a continuing re-evaluation of the design of the order-processing system in order for both to meet internal needs of the organisation and to take advantage of new options which become available.

From an internal operating perspective, information systems planning is the most important variable in controlling the quality of service. The dilemma is that distribution management normally has only limited familiarity with this area. However, improvement in service must involve them in information systems planning because it determines the way in which their own systems perform.

References

1. Bernard J. LaLonde and Paul H. Zinszer, *Customer Service: Meaning and Measurement* (Chicago: National Council of Physical Distribution Management, 1976).

4 The customer's perceptions of customer service

The question which is seldom asked in dealing with the problem of customer service is, how does the customer perceive the service that he is receiving. Management of customer service is often focused on a limited set of dimensions which are presumed to fit the needs of customers. If customers are asked about service, the survey instrument appears to follow along these same prescribed dimensions.

In this chapter, we will endeavour to enlarge the scope of the discussion by asking customers about their perceptions of customer service in a less structured way. Specifically the chapter will focus in turn on these questions:

1 How does the customer perceive customer service? More specifically, how are competitive service offerings of different suppliers evaluated and how is this evaluation influenced by differing role positions within the customer's organisation perceived?

2 How does he value customer service compared to other sources of influence by the manufacturer?

3 How does he value the individual components of customer service, both compared to other elements and also when compared to non-service elements in the sales transaction?

The project was begun with anticipation of being able to analyse customer service performance in comparison to measures of market performance. While several of the participating companies subscribed to market audit service which provided data on market performance, there was no corresponding data on customer services. This, however, led to other approaches which in the end may be more productive. The conventional wisdom of customer service is limiting. Customers may not necessarily react to order cycle time or its variability when they have specific problems in other areas. The simplest approach to the problem is then to ask directly about the elements of customer service which they feel to be important.

How do customers perceive service? Within the logistics system there may be a closed loop in operation. Distribution managers and receiving warehousemen have been trained to recognise order cycle time, and its variability, product availability and related factors as the dominant element of customer service. Only when other members of the customer's organisation are asked do different types of answers appear. These answers may be more broadly defined than logistics activities alone, and may include the entire interface between customer and supplier. Collectively they establish an impression within the customer's organisation of the supplier and his performance at a level where buying decisions are made.

What determines these perceptions? There appear to be two major influences: the organisation and the role position of the respondent. In contrast to much of the discussion in the literature, there may be substantial differences among customers as to what is desirable about suppliers' service. This results from the orientation of the customer within its industry, its organisational structure with its measurement and reward system, its reporting and hierarchical relationships; or it may result from the market position of the buyer relative to suppliers. Dominant firms in a buyer's market tend to have high expectations of supplier performance which obviously differ from those of weaker competitors. These in turn differ from those in a seller's market where the customer must assume the burdens normally supplied under the term 'service'.

The role position of the individual respondent also influences the response. Buyers are often specialised in their task activities by product class and possibly by vendor groups. Their responses can be expected to differ from operational managers or store branch managers, simply because of the decision-making perspectives and the level of information to which they have access. These responses will differ in turn from warehouse managers or credit managers for the same reasons. The result is that expressions of organisational perceptions are the responses of individuals which, because of their unique vantage points, may not reflect the collective decision-making response of the organisation.

The purpose of this chapter is to examine how customers perceive service, to probe the nature of the dimensions of service as these customers have determined them, and finally to establish the relative worth of these dimensions in the respondents' minds. The underlying theses are (1) that customer service is seen in less mechanistic terms than the conventional view would indicate, and (2) that specific valuations can be determined which are potentially the basis of supplier service strategies. The data presented here are the results of research with three of the companies in the project. These companies were selected because they provided the opportunity to explore specific aspects of the problem and did not present difficult data-collection tasks. Rather than present a complete compilation of all survey results, the findings shown here have been selected to demonstrate specific aspects of the problem.

How differently do customers perceive customer service?

Recognising the collective interpretation of the supplier's service within the customer's organisation is crucial to understanding the effectiveness of the service being offered. Perceptions of service will vary among customer organisations and by position within the organisation. The added concern is how these perceptions differ. Which dimensions of service are important to which customers and which of these dimensions holds the highest priority? Judgements about the characteristics of the market are only possible if there is some commonality of response. Conversely, if customers express divergent views, the management question turns on whether these are meaningful. Can customers be divided into different groups as separate market segments [3]? Should different services and communications be provided to meet the requirements of individual role positions within the organisation? Both of these should be of concern in developing effective strategies.

Research design

This issue of differential perception was explored in research cooperation with a major food products manufacturer dealing with the grocery trade. Supplying the market were five companies of unequal size. The firm in question held a significant second-place share. The products were in a well-defined class, with little substitution by consumers with other products outside this class. While the industry made noticeable efforts to achieve product differentiation, there was considerable brand switching taking place within the product market. Therefore, the key element in marketing strategy was to sustain access to the grocer's shelf, which required gaining and maintaining the support of major retail food chains.

The research plan involved calling on buyers, store division managers, store managers and warehouse managers of major food chains. The sample was designed to achieve representative market characteristics and not for statistical inference to larger populations.

A standardised interview approach was developed which permitted comparability of results. Each respondent was asked for four specific items of information:

1   a rank-ordering of suppliers within the product class in terms of customer service
2   a listing of criteria used in making these evaluations
3   a rank-ordering of these criteria in order of importance
4   a rank-ordering of each supplier against these individual criteria.

The respondent was completely free to develop his own criteria, although the interview attempted to focus on physical distribution service. This approach permitted the customer to define service in his own terms. By ranking both the suppliers and the criteria on which these suppliers were judged, the actual evaluations of suppliers could be compared to performance on elements which the respondent said were important. In this way, both the consistency of the evaluation and the potential dominance of specific elements of service could be established.

The data was then presented in simple rank-order terms which could be evaluated using rank-order correlation coefficients and a rank-order cluster analysis technique [2]. The output of the analysis for each respondent was:

1   a rank-order evaluation for each supplier in terms of service as the respondent defined it
2   a rank-ordered list of factors in order of priority which in effect defined customer service as the respondent perceived it, along with his ostensible basis for evaluating these suppliers
3   a rank-ordered list of suppliers for each attribute, in effect establishing their relative performance on that dimension of service
4   from the analysis, a measure of association (the Spearman rank-order correlation coefficient) between the overall supplier evaluation and each of the factors and also among the factors themselves.

Not all respondents felt themselves capable of making all of the judgements necessary. However, enough were able to do so to illustrate the problem. This approach however had another benefit, in that it provided a useful structure for further comments by the respondent. This could then be applied to enhance the basic data.

The perceived importance of customer service factors

Organisations might be expected to hold differing views on what constitutes customer service by suppliers. To make comparison possible, the rank orders of attributes in order of importance as expressed by buyers of retail food chains were used. There is, however, a common pattern which is shown in Table 4.1 which lists these service attributes in order of importance.

Table 4.1 Rank-ordering of factors perceived by head office buyers as important in evaluation of customer service

Variable	Index value
Product availability	60
Promotional activity	45
Representation	35
Order status	24
Distribution: direct or via depot	24
Delivery time	16
Pricing	16
Merchandising	15
Product positioning	15
Invoice accuracy	4
New product introduction	3
Advertising	1

For method of calculation, see text

This ranking was developed by identifying the number of times each ranking was mentioned and its rank. The individual rank orders were then averaged and converted into a scale from 1 to 10. This scale was then multiplied by the number of times mentioned. The Table is useful for identifying the most prominent dimensions, but the reader is cautioned about extending its use to individual comparisons.

'Product availability' clearly stands out as the dominant issue. Surprisingly, the next two items, 'promotional activity' and 'representation', are not a part of physical distribution, although they are part of the elements of the marketing mix. The three that follow, 'order status', 'direct versus indirect delivery' and 'delivery time', are a part of physical distribution.

'Delivery time' appears to be low in priority. The buyers as a group also do not separate physical distribution activities from other elements in the marketing mix. Individual responses are shown in Table 4.2. Two wholesalers were also included in this survey. Their results showed 'product availability' and 'delivery time' alternatively in first or second place.

The role of the respondent in the buying organisation is also important in determining which factors appear on the response. In Table 4.3 the responses of buyers and other managers involved in the supplier interface for two retail chains, one grocery wholesaler and three branch store managers are compared. Buyers appear to perceive the service offerings differently, from other members of their organisation, stressing 'product availability' more heavily than do other members of their organisation. There appears to be little pattern to these answers, except that the factors listed appear to be directly related to their own role positions in the organisation. 'Delivery time reliability' appears to be important but not consistently across the board.

The research design, it will be recalled, asked respondents to rank-order suppliers in an overall sense, and then to rank-order them in terms of the service elements that the respondent had previously listed as criteria. These rank-orders could then be compared to each other using Spearman rank correlation coeffients.* These coefficients were then used as the inputs to a matrix, a table of correlations which served to indicate how closely each of the elements used in the evaluation produced rank-order listings in comparison to one another. A high correlation measure indicates a high degree of association. The matrix then indicates a clustering of variables, including the overall rating, by degree of association.

The results of this analysis indicated that only in about half of the cases was the overall rating highly correlated with one of the elements listed in the rank-ordering. The element most frequently mentioned was 'delivery time', which is presumed to

---

* The use of the Spearman rank-correlation coefficient might be questioned in a rigorous application with a sample of such small size. The purpose here was to identify only the most prominent elements in the evaluation structure.

Table 4.2 Variables used for evaluation of customer service by head office buyers for multiples and cooperatives in rank order of imporance

Variable	Individual buyers							Times mentioned	Avg. rank	Index*
	A	B	C	D	E	F	G			
Product availability	1		1	2	3	2	1	6	1.67	60
Delivery time reliability	2	4						2	3	16
Invoice accuracy			3		8			2	5.5	4
Promotional activity	6			1	2	3	2	5	2.8	45
Representation	5	3			4	2	3	5	3.4	35
Information on order			4			1	4	3	3.0	24
Pricing	3	2			7		5	4	4.2	16
Distribution: direct/indirect			2		3	4	6	4	3.75	24
Merchandising				3	9	4		3	4	15
Product positioning and		1			1		7	3	4	15
Product introduction					5			1	5	3
Advertising					6			1	6	1

* See text

mean the time elapsed since placement of the order. In the other half, the overall rating on service has showed substantially less correlation (r = less than 0.7) with any single element. Here again the most frequently associated element with the overall rating was speed of delivery. However, this was only given low priority in the overall listing of elements in Table 4.1. Conversely some of the more highly-rated elements are not closely correlated with the overall rating.

One of the surprising results for several cases was the complete irrelevance of some of the identified elements in the matrix of the overall rating. For one buyer, representation at the head office and product quality were the most highly-correlated elements. The overall rating, however, was most closely associated with delivery speed. Pricing and representation at the store level were completely unrelated to the overall rating, even though the buyer had ranked them second and third in his own order of priority.

The importance of customer service elements varies by organisation and by position within the organisation. Product availability would appear to be the most important element in the buyers' lists of evaluating factors. Other factors become more important when other respondents are used. However, when the actual ratings of suppliers are compared to evaluation of performance on specific elements which the buyers named, the most important was delivery time. From this it is unclear where the major differentiation takes place: at an abstract level where factors are listed, detached from the suppliers, or at the individual supplier evaluation level.

How important is customer service?

In deciding on the level of resource commitment to customer service, the critical question is the degree of importance of customer service to the firm, in comparison to other elements

Table 4.3 Comparison by buying levels within the customer organisation of variables serving as a basis for evaluating customer service

| | Buying level by organisation | | | | | | | | |
| | Retail Chain A | | | Retail Chain B | | | Wholesaler | | |
	Head office buyer	Branch manager	Distribution manager	Buyer 1	Branch controller	Buyer 2	Buyer	Asst. dept. manager	Invoice manager
Product availability	1			1		1	2		
Delivery time reliability		4	2	2	4	3	1	1	
Delivery time average	3	3	3			2			
Representation	5	1	4	5	3				
Pricing	4			3	2				
Information			5						
Merchandising				4					
Promotional activity	2	2		6					
Handling ease			1		1				
Product range				7					
Distribution: direct or via depot	6								
Timing of complaints							3		
Invoice accuracy								2	
Packaging								3	1

in the marketing mix. If customers perceive it to be important, it should be emphasised. Otherwise, there is not much point in improving service performance beyond a minimal acceptable level.

Research design

One of the companies in the project, a manufacturer of small consumer durable goods, was concerned about a decline in market share and believed that service might be major factor in the decline. A decision was made as part of the project to undertake a survey of 32 of its dealers, in cooperation with their market research group.* Dealers were chosen to be representative both of size and region of the country, but were not selected at random.

The survey was developed in seven parts, two of which will be discussed later. The research discussed here will cover the first 5 parts. These are:

1   Details of the retail outlet including location, size both in turnover and number of employees, the number and names of other suppliers and the type of outlet. This was to provide a potential basis for segmentation, but the approach did not appear to be fruitful.

2   An open-ended question asking dealers to state the factors which they felt were important in buying from suppliers in this trade, and if possible to rank them in order of importance.

3   Dealers were then asked to examine a list of nine factors (shown on cards):

    a   market popularity of the brand
    b   condition on delivery
    c   the number of customer complaints
    d   advertising and promotional support
    e   product quality
    f   credit availability

---

* Data for this section was collected and analysed by the market research group of one of the sponsoring companies, and Mr David Reaves.

g   spare parts service
h   delivery and supply performance
i   discounts negotiated with manufacturers.

They were to take these nine and any other factors which they had mentioned independently and again order them by rank.

4   A set of 21 items concerning supplier-dealer relationships were shown to each dealer, asking him to respond on a five-point scale from 'excellent' to 'bad' for each of his suppliers, which yielded data on the perceived performance of each supplier and the industry average.

5   As a check on the questionnaire, dealers were asked to identify those areas of performance for each supplier that he was 'best at' and 'worst at'. A supplier might score heavily on all questions and still have a 'fatal flaw' in his performance.

The results

The rank orders of the unprompted lists from Part 2 were compared to the previously selected list in Part 3. For the modal values of the unprompted lists, the correlation with the selected list Part 3 was quite high (r = .92). The actual lists and rank orders are shown in Table 4.4.

Quality is obviously the most important factor in choosing suppliers. Delivery/availability was second on the prompted list, but is sufficiently close to spares and discounts to make all three approximately equivalent in ranking. Delivery is thus an important factor to these dealers. Any failure in delivery then should influence their choice of suppliers strongly. Advertising in this market is not among the top five factors, and appears to be irrelevant to dealers in some markets. Complaints from customers, credit and condition on delivery appear last, which may not indicate their real importance; dealers may not be having problems with trade credit, or they do not wish to discuss credit in a market survey.

Dealers were asked to use the 21 scaled items in the questionnaire to rate each supplier. An average rating for all suppliers was then used to describe overall industry performance. These results are shown in Table 4.5. Interestingly, industry performance tends to be high in product-related items such as 'quality of product', 'value for money' (3), 'complaints from customers' (4) and 'range of products' (5). Therefore among the list of items in the previous discussion, the first-ranked provides little basis for discrimination. However, items relating to questions of delivery and supply were ranked low in performance: 'accuracy of promised delivery dates' (13), 'information regarding orders and accounts' (17), 'order to delivery time' (18), 'availability from stocks' (19), and 'response to special requests' (20).

Table 4.4 Factors perceived by dealers to be important in dealing with suppliers

Rank	Unprompted Factors	Prompted Factors	Prompted
1	Quality	Quality	2.36
2	Spares	Delivery	3.78
3	Discount	Discount	4.40
4	Delivery	Spares	4.48
5	Popularity of bikes	Popularity	4.85
6	Advertising	Condition on Delivery	5.27
7	Condition on Delivery	Advertising Support	6.48
8	Complaints from Customers	Complaints from Customers	6.78
9	Credit	Credit	8.05

The sponsoring company was evaluated compared to other suppliers. In general, the firm (noted for this comparison as 'Alpha') was exceedingly strong in product quality, advertising, better product range, credit, information provided by sales representatives. However it was poor in accuracy of delivery dates, availability from stock, and response to special requests. In terms of general standing among the trade, 'Alpha' was clearly the worst. These results

Table 4.5 Aspects of service provided by suppliers as evaluated by dealers
Scale = 1 – excellent to 5 – extremely poor

Item	Overall performance rank	Overall	Alpha	Competitor 1	Competitor 2	Competitor 3	Competitor 4
Discount from manufacturers	14	2.73	2.69	2.72	2.50	2.94	3.11
Condition of goods when received	9	2.53	2.69	2.78	2.12	2.27	2.33
Value for money of product	3	2.43	2.51	2.11	2.12	3.05	1.89
Advertising/Promotional help	21	3.06	2.30	3.56	3.13	2.61	3.89
Range of products offered	5	2.52	1.52	3.00	3.00	2.72	3.00
Spares service	12	2.69	2.42	3.06	2.38	2.56	2.68
Accuracy of promised delivery date	13	2.76	2.97	2.94	2.88	2.61	2.78
Info. re. goods on order	10	2.89	2.64	3.22	2.88	2.94	2.78
Ease of placing orders and gen. trading	2	2.32	2.12	2.56	2.50	2.50	2.22
Information regarding accounts	17	2.61	2.27	3.06	2.50	2.94	2.56
Order to delivery time	18	2.91	3.15	3.11	3.13	2.50	2.67
Availability from stocks	19	2.93	3.03	3.06	3.38	2.61	3.00
Credit facilities	16	2.92	2.24	2.89	3.25	2.50	3.33
Response to special requests	20	3.00	3.12	2.72	2.63	3.11	2.89
Complaints from customers	4	2.51	2.64	2.78	2.13	2.78	2.33
General standing in trade	5	2.52	2.79	2.67	2.00	2.17	2.33
Profitability from suppliers	15	2.81	2.73	2.83	2.63	3.06	2.89
Day of delivery	8	2.55	2.12	2.89	2.75	2.77	2.56
Reps. frequency of call	9	2.60	2.12	2.89	3.25	2.77	2.89
Reps. info. on marketing development	11	2.67	2.12	3.17	3.00	2.56	2.67
Quality of products	1	2.16	2.18	2.11	1.63	2.22	2.33

indicate that within an industry in which delivery-related performance is weak, 'Alpha' was the worst in the industry, and this failure is instrumental in determining the overall trading image of the company among the dealers.

These observations were combined into a set of more condensed dimensions through factor analysis. Essentially, factor analysis attempts to draw out the underlying structure of the observed pattern of response, grouping together those questions which respondents have answered in similar ways. These groups are identified as 'factors'. The number of dimensions generated by the computer program depends on the degree of fit and the judgement of the analyst. Technically, the form of analysis used here is known as 'oblique rotation', indicating that the factors which are identified here are not completely independent of each other. This was done for ease of interpretation of the data.

The output of the analysis is a series of factors which are identified with specific groups of items on the basis of the contribution of that question to the pattern of response denoted by that factor. This contribution for each item and factor, is designated as a 'factor loading'. These loadings are then multiplied by the supplier's individual ratings, a measure of how each supplier is evaluated on each factor.

In Table 4.6, the factor analysis is presented, showing the five factors which have emerged from the data. The five factors and the contributing items are shown below:

1 *contact with dealer* (representatives' frequency of calls; ease of general trading; day of delivery)
2 *general standing in trade* (quality; complaints from customers; response to special requests; general standing in trade)
3 *pricing* (profitability from manufacturer; discounts; value for money)
4 *delivery* (order to delivery time; availability from stock; special requests; accuracy of promised delivery dates)
5 *back-up services* (advertising; range of products; spares; credit; representatives' information on market development)

These items did not combine into distinct factors: condition of goods when received; information regarding goods on order and information regarding accounts.

Table 4.6 Factor analysis of service provided by suppliers as evaluated by dealers

(1) Factor loadings					
Factors	X_1	X_2	X_3	X_4	X_5
Item					
Discount from manufacturers			.34		
Condition of goods when received					
Value for money of product			.30		
Advertising/promotional help					.25
Range of products offered					.22
Spares service					.21
Accuracy of delivery date				.40	
Info re. goods on order					
Ease of placing orders and general trading	.34				
Information regarding accounts					
Order to delivery time				.37	
Availability from stocks				.31	
Credit facilities					.19
Response to special requests		.24			
Complaints from customers		.24			
General standing in trade		.23			
Profitability from suppliers			.36		
Day of delivery	.31				
Reps' frequency of call	.35				
Reps' info on marketing development					.17
Quality of products		.28			

Factor scores of the individual suppliers are calculated by multiplying the factor loadings in Table 4.6 by the original scores on the individual items in Table 4.5. These are calculated for individual items and combined for a total factor score in Table 4.7.

In total score, 'Alpha' was the lowest rated (i.e. the *most* preferred) supplier. Its particular areas of strength according to the factor scores are in the areas of market contact and

Table 4.7 Factor analysis of service provided by suppliers as evaluated by dealers

	(2) Factor scores				
	Alpha	Competitor 1	Competitor 2	Competitor 3	Competitor 4
Factor 1 — Contact					
Reps' freq. of call	0.74	1.01	1.13	0.97	1.01
Ease of gen. trading	0.72	0.87	0.85	0.85	0.76
Day of delivery	0.66	2.78	2.83	2.68	2.57
	2.12	2.78	2.83	2.68	2.57
Factor 2 — General standing in trade					
Quality	0.61	0.59	0.46	0.62	0.65
Complaints from customers	0.64	0.68	0.51	0.68	0.56
Response to special requests	0.75	0.65	0.63	0.75	0.69
Gen. standing in trade	0.64	0.61	0.46	0.50	0.53
	2.64	2.53	2.06	2.55	2.43
Factor 3 — Pricing					
Profitability from manuf.	0.98	1.01	0.94	1.10	1.04
Discounts	0.92	0.92	0.85	1.00	1.06
Value for money	0.75	0.63	0.64	0.92	0.57
	2.65	2.56	2.43	3.02	2.67
Factor 4 — Delivery					
Order to delivery time	1.17	1.13	1.15	0.93	0.99
Availability from stock	0.95	0.94	1.04	0.81	0.93
Accuracy of promised del. date	0.92	0.91	0.89	0.81	0.86
	3.04	2.98	3.08	2.55	2.78
Factor 5 — Back-up					
Advertising	0.56	0.78	0.69	0.57	0.86
Range of products	0.33	0.66	0.66	0.60	0.66
Spares	0.51	0.64	0.50	0.54	0.56
Credit	0.43	0.55	0.62	0.48	0.63
Reps' info. on market devel.	0.36	0.54	0.51	0.43	0.45
	2.14	3.17	2.98	2.61	3.16
Total	12.59	14.02	13.38	13.41	13.61

back-up service, which probably reflects its size and resources available, compared to competitors, as well as strong management direction in these areas. The weakest areas are those of delivery and general standing in the trade. In delivery, 'Alpha' almost tied for last place among the five suppliers. In general trade standing, the item which has pulled their rating down has been response to special requests. In general, 'Alpha's' standing is ahead of competition because of strong sales force and product support, although its delivery performance is poor. Dealers, however, are highly sensitive to delivery performance and this is generally poor among all suppliers in the market. A programme to improve distribution service may achieve more response for Alpha than almost any other area of customer-dealer relations. The question is then: what type of service should 'Alpha' provide?

What aspects of customer service are most important to the customer?

Customer service is a product just as much as the physical product that the supplier offers. Some aspects of service are particularly valuable to customers. Others are of apparently little use. The problem is to find out which dimensions are most desirable and how much more than other dimensions.

There are several possible approaches to obtain answers to this problem. One way is to change specific aspects of service and see how the market responds. This of course is potentially dangerous for customer relations because it forces the customer to change his own operating system in response to experimental and possibly temporary changes in the supplier's system. It may also be ineffective in evoking response as the customer may not understand what is taking place, or may not wish to commit himself for temporary changes.

Another approach is to ask him. The survey approach is probably typical of current practice [1 and 4]. The customer responds to a series of questions, making preferential evaluations on aspects of service. While he may be potentially capable of providing accurate responses to those aspects of service which he has experienced, he may have no conception of service and its impact on his system beyond his own range of experience [4, p. 86]. This method also suffers from another disadvantage: survey responses involve low commitment because they are not related to real problems and decisions, i.e. no rewards for responses which turn out to be favourable or penalties for those that are not. Questions may also be asked out of context; delivery service may be referred to apart from other aspects of service, such as documentation or product availability.

Trade-off analysis

Recently another approach has been advocated: trade-off analysis. The original applications in marketing have come from consumer behaviour. However, it holds considerable promise in dealing with choices of service attributes.

The pioneering effort applying trade-off analysis to distribution is by Perrault and Russ [5]; only a brief description of the method will be used here. A customer may be faced with several different suppliers, each with different types of service, such as fast versus slow delivery, etc. He prefers one combination of service to another because it has more value to him, possibly, for example, in reducing his inventory costs. This value is identified as 'utility'. The objective in customer service is to identify those elements which can be offered to create the highest possible utility to the customer. The problem for the supplier is to determine how much utility is created if, for example, he offers faster delivery, and further how much more is that worth than maintaining a high standard of product availability, assuming that he has only limited resources.

Customers are presumed to choose suppliers from among a set with differing service offerings, the choice implying a valuation of these service attributes. In the actual application of trade-off analysis, the consumer is then faced with selecting the supplier with the most preferred combination of attributes. His preference then defines the utility of all of the service elements.

The algorithm used is Conjoint Analysis. The computer program MONANOVA transforms simple preferences into utilities, which are then summed for individual combinations. The objective is to substitute values of utility for simple preference rankings, while preserving the same rank order [5 p. 122]. The algorithm thus tries simultaneously to estimate overall utility and measures of utility of different service levels for each of the attributes involved. The process is iterative; the program proceeds in a stepwise fashion until there is no further change.

In applying MONANOVA as a form of trade-off analysis, there are several assumptions which should be noted. First, the interview situation presents a situation out of context. From that standpoint, it may not be realistic and the choices that the respondent makes may therefore also be unrealistic. Second, the valuations of the attributes are assumed to be linear and additive. Again this may not reflect individual value systems. Third, there is also a potential problem of failure to identify relevant dimensions to the problem. The respondent is forced to respond to dimensions which have been predetermined for him. To some extent, this can be overcome through careful pre-testing. There is no assurance, however, that the problem can ever be completely solved. Finally, the complexity of choice by respondents in dealing with problems with multiple attributes may lead to inaccurate judgements. While these are legitimate difficulties with the technique, the process is used here to provide tentative insights into the valuation of specific dimensions of service.

Application to appliance dealers

From preliminary conversation with dealers, four elements appeared to be the most relevant components of delivery and supply to them:

1   order to delivery time

2   information on their orders and accounts
3   the percentage of items on their orders available directly
     from stock
4   reliability of the delivery date

These were further divided into conditions that the dealer
could reasonably expect to take place:

1   order to delivery time
     a   within two weeks
     b   within four weeks
     c   within six weeks
2   information on orders
     a   no information
     b   regular information
3   the percentage of items on their orders available from
     stock*
     a   50 per cent from stock
     b   80 per cent from stock
4   the reliability of the delivery date
     a   the delivery date is usually reliable
     b   the delivery date is unreliable

The item 'special requests' was considered but was not used in
this analysis because of program limitations; it was included in
the rating list in the previous section.**

   From these attributes, a description of hypothetical suppliers
could be synthesised which would describe the range of services
available. For instance the following two hypothetical supply
situations will indicate the possibilities:

Supplier 1   4 weeks delivery
              reliable delivery dates
              no regular information on orders
              80 per cent of items from stock

---

* where an item was *not* in stock, dealers were told it would take eight weeks to arrive.

**Perrault and Russ used a price difference as one of the variables, thus establishing a
direct relationship between utility and monetary value. This was not done here
because of reluctance by the Sales Department to involve pricing issues directly in the
study.

Supplier 2   2 weeks delivery
              unreliable delivery date
              regular information supplied on orders
              80 per cent of items from stock

The possible combinations were 24 (3 × 2 × 2 × 2). This however is far too great a list for dealers to examine. By eliminating improbable combinations, the total list was reduced to nine. Each of the remaining 'suppliers' was then shown to the dealers as a single card. The dealer was then asked to rank these nine in an order preference.

The 'ideal' and the 'worst' cases being eliminated, the dealers by ranking were forced to evaluate good versus bad service in each of these elements as part of a total service 'package'. Each dealer was in effect asked to 'trade-off' the aspects of service that he wanted versus those about which he did not care so much.

Results

The output was a series of utility measures describing the relative values that each respondent places on each factor. The mean values of the 32 dealers were used to provide overall summary values which are analogous to utility values. While a few outlying values were included in the process, the vast majority conformed closely to this average, which is partly a result of the constrained choices open to these dealers in the interview. These values are shown below:

Order to delivery time:
  2 weeks   + 12.64
  4 weeks   + 2.37
  6 weeks   − 15.11
Reliability of delivery times:
  reliable   + 15.39
  unreliable − 15.39
Products available from stock:
  80 per cent + 7.64
  50 per cent − 7.64

Information on orders:
  regular   + 5.42
  irregular   − 5.42
A positive score indicates that the dealer prefers that particular level of service; the higher the score, the stronger the preference. A negative score indicates a desire to avoid that service level. Thus in this case, reliability appears to be the most important element, followed by order-to-delivery time (order cycle time), availability from stock and regularity of information in that order.

The usefulness of this information lies not only in the indication of preference of one dimension of service over another, but also the degree of preference. For example, 2 weeks delivery is worth 12.64 units, while six weeks delivery is worth a minus 15.11. A dealer being asked to consider different service packages would have to be compensated by 27.75 units of utility to shift from two weeks delivery to six weeks and be no worse off than before.

To demonstrate this, the nine combinations which were considered by the dealers are listed with their total scores, in Table 4.8. A combination with 4 weeks delivery, reliability, 80 per cent of the order filled from stock and regular information has a score of + 30.82, which is better than the next alternative of 2 weeks delivery, reliability, and regular information but with only 50 per cent of the order being filled from stock. The dealer in effect has sacrificed 10.27 units of utility by accepting the slower delivery time, but gained 15.28 units from the gain in the proportion of the order filled from stock. The dealer by choosing the highest-rated combination has selected from his options in alternative suppliers to maximise his utility. These measures can then be used to consider different alternative service packages to determine which ones are most desirable.

The problem of aggregating data for all dealers will now be reconsidered. Averaging suggests that this dealer sample might be subdivisible into groups with specific service preferences. The dealers as an intermediate market might be segmented into specific groups based on unique preferences for different combinations of customer service. To test this, a cluster analysis using rank-order correlations was tried, but was unsuccessful. The dealer sample may be so heterogeneous that average data reasonably represents customer service preference in the absence of strong and pronounced distinctions among segments.

Table 4.8 Mean evaluation of test combinations of attributes used in *MONANOVA* customer service survey

Rank	Score	Service dimensions			
		Order time	Reliability	% from stock	Information
1	+ 30.82	4 weeks	Yes	80%	Regular
2	+ 25.82	2 weeks	Yes	50%	Regular
3	+ 4.70	4 weeks	Yes	50%	Irregular
4	+ 2.50	6 weeks	Yes	80%	Irregular
5	+ 0.04	4 weeks	No	80%	Regular
6	− 0.53	2 weeks	No	80%	Irregular
7	− 15.81	2 weeks	No	50%	Irregular
8	− 28.28	6 weeks	No	80%	Irregular
9	− 32.72	6 weeks	No	50%	Regular

Another application and results

Another supplier of consumer durables in this project experienced problems in customer service. The company shall be referred to as 'Beta' during this discussion. In this particular market, sales were highly seasonal; the sales year was characterised by several seasons for different parts of the product line. Sales were made in large part through stock shows where dealers went to examine the product line and place orders. Dealers in this industry would normally place up to half of their orders at the show. The remainder would be ordered directly by the dealer or through a salesman calling on the shop.

The research design originally was planned for extended interviews with 30 dealers in south-east England. The geographic area was important to the company in terms of sales. Dealer relationships here would be critical to maintaining national sales volume. The Domestic Sales manager also stated that he found little difference except in the total volume of business between the area and the rest of the country. Because of difficulties in gaining access to dealers, the number of actual interviews completed was 26.

The survey instrument was a questionnaire which asked about the size of the shop, their purchasing behaviour (whether they tended to emphasise stock show orders or ordering from their own shops afterwards) the types of shows preferred, patterns of ordering, preferences on average order size and their experience in deliveries from 'Beta'.

The service provided by 'Beta' was evaluated on nine factors determined both through informal conversation with dealers and the specific points of interest of the Sales manager. These were:

1 delivery time from order placement
2 consistency of delivery
3 information about orders
4 credit
5 convenience of invoicing
6 minimum order policy
7 condition of goods on arrival
8 ease of returns
9 special requests.

Respondents were asked to evaluate performance on a five-point scale comparing 'Beta' to the average of other suppliers. The dimensions on which 'Beta' were rated highest were credit, the condition of goods on arrival and special requests. The areas of weakest performance were the minimum order policy, delivery time and information about goods on order. Respondents were asked to identify the most important and least important dimensions of service to them. Most important was time of delivery, which was the worst area of perceived performance. Next was consistency of delivery. Least important was minimum order size, followed by the convenience of the invoice form. 'Beta's' service image to customers appears to be determined by the speed of delivery. The second most important element, consistency, is evaluated more positively. The weakest element is information, both on stock availability and order status once the order is placed. This however appears to be a general weakness across this particular industry.

The research of most interest here is two applications of conjoint analysis using the MONANOVA algorithm. The first was concerned with stock show ordering and delivery practice, the second with replenishment ordering at the shop. These analyses demonstrate the interrelationship between physical distribution and sales activities, that delivery and sales policies are not always separable issues.

Considering the stock show problem first, a set of three issues were selected as a result of discussion with the sales manager.

These and the allowable choice of service levels are:
Order placement:
   Place at the show
   Place at the shop
Take delivery:
   within one month after order placement
   within three months after order placement
Order completion:
   within one month after initial delivery
   within three months after initial delivery
A typical combination might include:
   placing the order at the show
   taking delivery within one month
   completing the order within three months
another would be:
   placing the order at the show
   taking delivery within three months
   completing the order within one month

The results of the stock show MONANOVA run indicated:
(1)	Ordering at the show	+ 0.63
	Ordering at the shop	− 0.63
(2)	Delivery within one month	− 1.48
	Delivery within three months	+ 1.48

(3)   Completion of the order in one
       month following delivery
       completion of the order in three
       months following delivery   -0.63

Taking the first example,
   Ordering at the show   + 0.63
   Delivery in one month   − 1.48
   Completing in three months   − 0.63
                                        ───────
                                        − 1.48

The second is,
   Placing an order at the show   + 0.63
   Taking delivery in three months   + 1.48
   Completing the order in one month   + 0.63
                                        ───────
                                        + 2.74

The second is preferred to the first. A complete enumeration of
the possible choices and their indicated utilities is shown in
Table 4.9. What the utility numbers indicate is that in this
case, dealers prefer an extended period before the first
delivery, which is logical, given the context within which orders
are placed. Stock shows are several months in advance of the
season. Dealers know that if they receive shipment early,
standard credit terms will force them to pay early. Equal
weight is given to the other issues of where to order and how
long to complete the order.

The second MONANOVA analysis involved these options
for replenishment orders:
Dealers prefer delivery in
   one week
   four weeks
Dealers would prefer orders be filled with
   50 per cent of items from stock
   80 per cent of items from stock
Dealers prefer that balance (back) orders be held
   permanently in file
   held for three months and then dropped
Dealers prefer to have order status information
   every two weeks
   every six months.

Table 4.9 Ordering preference combinations using
MONANOVA analysis

Alternative	Dimension	Component values	Total value
1	Delivery 3 months	+ 1.48	
	Completion 1 month	+ 0.63	
	Order at show	+ 0.63	+ 2.74
2	Delivery 3 months	+ 1.48	
	Completion 1 month	+ 0.63	
	Order at shop	− 0.63	+ 1.48
3	Delivery 3 months	+ 1.48	
	Completion 3 months	− 0.63	
	Order at show	+ 0.63	+ 1.48
4	Delivery 3 months	1.48	
	Completion 3 months	− 0.63	
	Order at shop	− 0.63	+ 0.22
5	Delivery 1 month	− 1.48	
	Completion 1 month	+ 0.63	
	Order at show	+ 0.63	− 0.22
6	Delivery 1 month	− 1.48	
	Completion 1 month	+ 0.63	
	Order at shop	− 0.63	− 1.48
7	Delivery 1 month	− 1.48	
	Completion 3 months	− 0.63	
	Order at show	+ 0.63	− 1.48
8	Delivery 1 month	− 1.48	
	Completion 3 months	− 0.63	
	Order at shop	− 0.63	− 2.74

The results for the majority of dealers indicated
overwhelmingly (73 per cent) a preference for fast delivery over
the 80 per cent proportion of items filled from stock. This is
consistent with comments from dealers who were asking the
supplier 'Give us something to sell, even if the completed order
takes longer'. The balance order and order information
variables had zero values in the computer printout, indicating
that delivery and the proportion of items from stock completely
dominated their choices. The actual values for the most

frequently expressed trade-off preferences were:

Delivery within one week	+ 1.90
Delivery within four weeks	− 1.90
Stock availability 80 per cent	+ 0.63
Stock availability 50 per cent	− 0.63

Table 4.10 Replenishment ordering preference combinations using *MONANOVA* analysis

Alternative	Dimensions	Component values	Total value
1	Delivery one week	+ 1.90	
	80% stock availability	+ 0.63	+ 2.53
2	Delivery one week	+ 1.90	
	50% stock availability	− 0.63	+ 1.27
3	Delivery four weeks	− 1.90	
	80% stock availability	+ 0.63	− 1.27
4	Delivery four weeks	− 1.90	
	50% stock availability	− 0.63	− 2.53

The list of combinations and their values is shown in Table 4.10. The important point from this is that delivery in one week with 50 per cent stock availability is preferred to four weeks with 80 per cent.

The findings of this research were dictated by the ordering practices within this particular market and also by the characteristically slow delivery of this industry. Service is apparently poor among all suppliers, although some dealers mentioned small competitors who were responding quickly, capitalising on the slower response of larger competitors.

In comparison to the previous analysis, the market for 'Beta' is less well-defined than 'Alpha's'. No competitor competes with 'Beta' across the full product range, so that suppliers cannot be compared on a uniform basis.

The lack of experience with good service makes the dealers less responsive to options in service which they have not tried. If service were to improve, it is possible that these dealers would be better 'educated' in the potential of service to reduce their own costs.

Discussion

The major difficulty in measuring customer perception of suppliers' service is a lack of common agreement on what is being perceived. Only on fundamental physical distribution management dimensions, such as average delivery time, variability in delivery time, product availability, is there a common ground. These measurements tend to keep customer service within a narrowly defined system which may be controllable and commonly recognised, but can be a relatively minor area in the larger arena of providing service at the customer-supplier interface. Service is defined differently by individual customer organisations and according to the specific role position of the respondent.

For the most effective response, service should be emphasised where it is most influential in maintaining sales, recognising that some parts of the organisation may not influence vendor selection decisions. However, once the central decision-maker is identified, it becomes relevant to ask 'who else can influence the decision?'. Service appears to deal with several different points in the organisation simultaneously which may contribute to the final decision. Finally, of these potential points of influence, what is their relative importance?

The findings presented here for the food manufacturer do not involve the influence network, although they do emphasise the variety of differences in perspective of differing role positions. The other research was simpler in scope, dealing almost exclusively with small shops and individual owner-managers. The choice of subjects was deliberate to eliminate the role position as an influencing variable.

One purpose of this chapter has been to explore the contribution of research to answering the question: what elements are important to the customer service mix? Beyond actually experimenting in the market, this research must ask questions about an intangible product — the service system. Unless the customer rationally monitors this system, evaluation is likely to be determined through singular events. In a sense, evaluation is asymetric; service which meets expectations is taken for granted, service which is bad forms distinct impressions.

Service is situation-specific. The 'Beta' company's situation is entirely different from 'Alpha's'. One firm manages ordering as a process, which takes place over most of the year. The other deals with ordering as a series of cyclical 'events', the stock shows, to be followed by replenishment orders. There do not appear to be general rules about service levels, because every market is unique. Practices are tied to buying procedures, past history, the level of competition and how service is integrated into competitive actions. In some industries such as the one in which 'Beta' operates, service has traditionally been low. Many aspects of service such as order status reporting to customers are unknown.

A high level of service may invite retaliation in return for a short-term competitive advantage. The result is a reluctance to increase service if the effects of massive increases in expenditure will be nullified. However, how long will a low-level equilibrium continue before the pressures to improve are unleashed in the market?

The possibility of segmentation was mentioned briefly early in the discussion. In a sense, most firms have practised segmentation in providing special treatment for large customer accounts. The real test of the interest in this concept will come when customers with distinctly different patterns of service response and order-placement behaviour are treated uniquely through specifically planned service packages.

References

1. Bender, Paul S., *Design and Operation of Customer Service Systems* (New York: AMACOM, 1976).
2. Elliott, Ken and Martin Christopher, *Research Methods in Marketing*, (London: Holt, Rinehart and Winston, 1974) pp. 194-198.
3. Gilmour, Peter, 'Customer Service: Differentiating by Marketing Segment', *International Journal of Physical Distribution*, Vol.7, No.3 (1977), pp.141-149.

4. Hutchinson, William M. and John F. Stolle, 'How to Manage Customer Service,' *Harvard Business Review,* Vol.47 (Nov.-Dec. 1968), pp.85-96.
5. Perrault, William D. and Frederick A. Russ, 'Improving Physical Distribution Service Decisions with Trade-off Analysis', *International Journal of Physical Distribution,* Vol.7, No.3 (1977) pp.117-127.

5 Customer service and the impact on the consumer[*]

Distribution of products to final consumers involves a chain of transactions resulting in the product being available at the point of final sale. Every event in the flow of goods has the power to influence whether the product is actually in stock at the point of sale or not.

Marketing strategies make the assumption that products will be available when needed. Strategies to produce new products, build brand loyalties and maintain market share, all imply high levels of distribution performance. Maintaining products in stock can become a major problem. Data however is scarce, although a study made in 1968 indicated that in supermarket retailing 11 per cent of potential sales were lost as a result of stock-outs of products on the store shelf [10]. The stock-out is the culmination of a chain of events taking place within the distribution system. Customer service is a series of interfaces, first between supplier and intermediary, between itnermediary and retailer and finally between retailer and consumer. Each of these points involves separate decision-making about inventory management and order policy. If the chain is broken anywhere in the system, and unless there is redundant stock in the system, the effects will utimately appear as a stock-out at the point of final sale. As profit margins are squeezed within the marketing channel, cost pressures on distribution and specifically finished goods inventory will increase.

---

*An earlier version of this chapter appears as 'The Anatomy of a Stockout' to be published in the *Journal of Retailing* (forthcoming).

At this point we are less concerned with the causes of stock-outs than with the impact of stock-outs on consumer choice. If the product is not on the shelf, what decisions do consumers make, and what impact then does a stock-out have on the marketing and financial performance of the firm? A stock-out may result in any of several alternative actions. First, the stock-out may be totally ignored or even unknown to the consumer. If the stock-out is recognised, does behaviour then represent only a temporary aberration in sales, or are there long-term consequences? Do these long-term consequences have their greatest impact on the supplier of the brand, or on the store?

Pressures on both suppliers and retailers to avoid stock-outs are severe. Buying practices among supermarket chains have tended to reduce the number of brands available in order to achieve higher turnover on the store shelf. At the same time, suppliers strive to maintain their brands in retail distribution as this becomes a key to access to the consumer market. Consumer brand choice, as Farley once noted, appears to be determined by the retailers' selection more than by consumers' individual preferences standing alone [4]. This makes the retailer buyer a pivotal figure in determining consumer brand choice [7]. According to a study by Shycon and Sprague [13], these buyers are prone to retaliate against suppliers who do not maintain a supply of their product to the customer, even to the point of refusing to stock new products which are being introduced. A failure of customer service to the retail buyer then has potential long-term implications extending beyond the individual product alone.

In this chapter, we are concerned with the effects of stock-outs on consumer decision-making as a measure of the effect of customer service. A model will be presented to identify specific aspects of the choice process for further investigation. Evidence will then be presented on specific issues raised. Finally, implications will be drawn for strategy options in distribution.

A Model of consumer stock-out behaviour

A model of consumer response to out-of-stock situations is shown in Figure 5.1 [8]. Behaviour caused by stock-outs leads to diversion or loss of patronage and future goodwill. In general, the stock-out can be expected to lead to a frustration of a purchase plan, caused by the inability to complete it. Ultimately it may begin to change the perception of the product, brand or store.

It contains four component modules, which are related through consumer and retailer response to stock-outs. These modules also include some autonomy of action. These are:

I Store and product decisions
II Consumer behaviour
III Response to out-of-stock situations
IV Retail merchandising strategy

The only areas of possible measurement are; the actual stock-out behaviour (III), and retail merchandising strategy (IV); the rest are implied. Nevertheless, inferences should be possible, based on the evidence of past and present behaviour.

The process is initiated by a consumer buyer with an assumed motivation to purchase a product (1). Through previously-held perceptions (2), attitudes are formed (3) leading to a decision to purchase a specific brand (4). At this point, the choice is directed to perceptions of the store (5) resulting in attitudes (6) leading to store choice (7). Included as a component of store image is an expectation of product availability based on store product assortment. This image is further augmented by anticipations of convenience in purchasing, derived from anticipation of finding the product within the store, speed of the check-out and possibly location.

Although a stock-out may be encountered in fact (8) it may not be observed by the consumer (9). Perception is related to the consumer's own shopping behaviour. Those with pre-planned shopping lists and strong brand preferences may have specific brands and sizes in mind. On the other hand, some consumers may specifically search for only a few items, relying

Figure 5.1 Process model of a stock-out

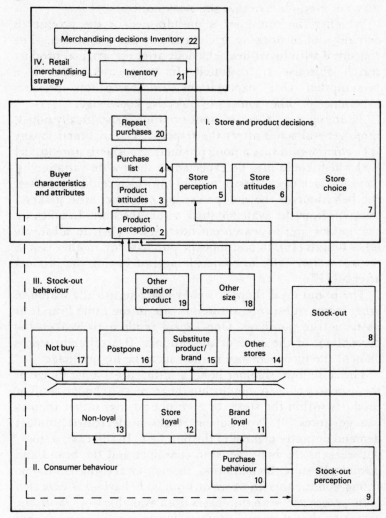

on the store as a 'memory bank' for the others; some consumers may not even observe that the stock-out exists.

Whether the consumer is misinformed or the product is actually out-of-stock is irrelevant for this discussion. The concern is with his or her behaviour after the original product search objective is frustrated. In most cases, there is a presumption that expectations are based on previous experience or other sources of objective knowledge.

Assuming that an out-of-stock situation is specifically noted, three general states affect the response. One is brand loyalty (11) which would vary among products. Another is store loyalty (12) which could also be expected to show wide variation. A third is a lack of expressed loyalty (13) which could also reflect the behaviour of the non-perceiving consumer who makes a selection from the available stock within the store. In all cases, the options are: to search out other stores (14), to substitute other brands (15), to postpone the purchase for another visit to the same store (16), or to decide against buying the product after all (17).

The brand-loyal shopper would characteristically search in other stores, substitute a different size in the same brand, or postpone the purchase. One logical result is to weaken the perceptions of the store or the product. If a different size is chosen, the inconvenience may weaken the brand image.

The store-loyal shopper holds a sufficiently strong image of the store to prefer to shop within the store, switching brands or products within the store, or even not buying, rather than to change stores [3]. Not buying results in decreased product demand or postponement of the purchase. In this case, a stock-out weakens the bond between consumer and the brand and possibly the store. By definition, the non-loyal consumer has no strong bonds either to stores or brands. Behaviour is expected to be pragmatic, with purchases from available stock, with the exception that store and product images may be so weak that they are not considered as even casual shopping choices. This consumer may comprise an important market segment, treating products and possibly stores as shopping and convenience goods [1].

Both consumer and marketer may expect perfect performance without interruption as a matter of course. Retail merchandising strategy and indirectly that of the manufacturer in this context is to reinforce repeat purchase behaviour. If adequate inventories of specific items cannot be maintained, this may ultimately lead to exclusion and substitution of the stocked-out item. Effective logistics performance can therefore contribute to the marketing mix as a positive influence, enabling product and store cues to operate on the consumer's choice.

The evidence of consumer stock-out behaviour

The number of published studies of stock-out behaviour involving consumers are few in number. The two most extensive have been performed by A. C. Neilsen; an American study summarised in *Progressive Grocer* in 1968 [6, 10]; and a 1974 study conducted in Britain, reported in the *Neilsen Researcher* [9]. In the British study, 2,558 consumers experiencing stock-outs in grocery stores were interviewed immediately upon leaving the store and asked about their purchase decisions.

Another approach was reported by Walter and Grabner [14] concerning consumers at a state-owned liquor store. They were asked about their intended hypothetical behaviour if confronted with a stock-out in the store. This approach, however, was questioned by D Walters who was involved wit the Neilsen study [5] noting substantial differences between intended and actual behaviour in stock-out situations.

The model suggests several potential hypotheses for which research might provide at least partial answers and which have significance for distribution strategy.

Hypothesis No.1:   *Consumers who perceive stock-outs differ in underlying characteristics from those who do not.* If consumers drawn from a different social class behave differently when encountering stock-outs, then the behaviour should be predictable from the background of store patrons. If stock-out incidence reports are higher for some groups rather than others, the stock-out itself takes on more significance in specific store locations rather than others and hence, regardless of the actual performance of the distribution system, may not be a universal problem.

Hypothesis No.2:   *Consumers who note that a specific brand is out of stock will search for that brand rather than substitute another, and this behaviour will vary depending on whether the customer is shopping for national or private brands*. The degree of brand loyalty will be manifested in the willingness to switch stores or substitute sizes rather than brands. Those asking for national brands would be presumed to be more inclined to shop in other stores for the brand than would shoppers for own-label brands. The intensity of brand loyalty, at least in the short run, may provide some buffering for distribution performance.

Hypothesis No.3:   *The image of the store is weakened as a result of encountering an out-of-stock situation*. Logically, an image of product availability would be weaker as a result; however, the images of ostensibly independent aspects of store image may also be affected. This would then place an onus on the store to ensure better service to avoid a lower evaluation of the store as an entity.

Hypothesis No.4:   *Stock-outs of products have a measurable effect on market share*. Stock-outs, particularly if widespread, should reduce market shares. This would take place because of (a) retailers who would switch patronage and (b) consumers, who in the past had developed a stimulus-response bonding with the product, now find that other products can substitute [11]. This is the direct pay-off for poor distribution service; hence it becomes a strong motivator for improved service to protect an established market position.

Research procedure

The principal evidence is drawn from a survey conducted at two units of a British supermarket chain. Both stores were located in suburban commuter communities near London. This chain is primarily patronised by families with the head of the household in a managerial or professional occupation. However, neither store was limited to this patronage alone.

Differences in occupational or age class distribution in patronage between the two stores were not significant. Further, the results, either in the incidence during or in the behaviour subsequent to stock-outs, were not markedly different. For the purpose of this study, the data from these two stores were combined.

The highest incidence of stock-out is logically experienced at peak store traffic times, which means Friday afternoon and evening and Saturday. For interviewing, two weekends were selected approximately one month apart. Interviewers were stationed near the cash registers, questioning shopprs just after leaving the check-out area. A shopper who did not find an item and left without buying would normally leave via the check-out area.

A total of 1,167 interviews was taken, of which 343 (or 29.4 per cent) reported experiencing one or more items being out-of-stock. The specific interest in the interview was in the post-stock-out behaviour. No attempt was made to measure the incidence of stock-outs experienced. Interviewers were instructed to obtain a quota of interviews involving response to stock-outs in addition to a reasonable number of interviews with those not experiencing stock-outs for comparison.

Respondents were asked whether they encountered an item to be out-of-stock, the identification of the item and their behaviour subsequent to the stock-out event. They were then asked to evaluate the store chain on a scale from 0 to 9 on seven specific dimensions which, from pre-survey interviews, were presumed to indicate components of their image towards the store. Finally, they were asked to state their age and occupation. These were grouped by categories which confirm to British census divisions for use: under 30, 30-44, 45-64, and 65 and over, and standard British social class notation identifying classes by the occupation of the head of the household: professional and managerial, office worker, skilled or semi-skilled worker, unskilled worker, retired and other.

The results

The first hypothesis suggested that consumers reporting stock-out incidents differed insignificantly from other shoppers interviewed. This was confirmed by data in the survey. Shoppers reporting out-of-stock incidents were predominantly in the 30-44 years age category and from families where the head of the household was in a managerial or professional occupation. (The x^2 levels of significance were less than 0.005 and 0.001 respectively.) Shoppers reporting stock-outs thus appear to differ in readily identifiable characteristics from those not reporting. Stores with heavy proportions of upper strata would tend to be more encumbered by reports of stock-outs than stores with different classes of patronage.

What actions do consumers take when they encounter stock-out situations? The focus of these data is branded-food items which accounted for almost 79 per cent of the items reported missing. The aggregate behaviour pattern is shown in Table 5.1.

More than one item could be reported in a single interview and the average was 1.27 items per report of stock-out. The overall performance in taking substitute actions appears to be generally similar to data reported in the Neilsen studies. However, the American Nielsen study noted distinct differences among different demographic categories. The American study identified five types of neighbourhood groups: high income, blue collar, Negroes, suburban middle income, and urban apartments. The proportion of customers who stated that they would buy elsewhere in that study varied from

32 per cent for the 'high income' group to 33 per cent for 'Negroes'. [10, p.25-31]. In our own study, the managerial-professional category showed a higher proportion (56.7 per cent) searching in other stores. Other studies report that stock-outs and post-stock-out behaviour also appear to vary substantially by store chain and by product area, which may also be related to characteristics of the shopper.

Table 5.1 Reported behaviour of shoppers experiencing stock-outs

Action taken	Number	Percentage
Bought same brand, different size	21	4.8
Bought different brand	22	5.0
Bought different product	54	12.4
Postponed purchase until next visit to same store	48	11.1
Decided not to buy	81	18.7
Decided to search in other stores	208	47.9
Total	434	100.0

Do patterns of brand loyalty influence stock-out behaviour? The second hypothesis distinguished between the stated intentions of national versus private brand purchasers. The particular chain in this study has a dominant share of its business in private brands, well-promoted and with an apparently strong quality image. Customers seeking these brands might be characterised here as 'store-loyal'. Those asking for other brands would then be 'brand-loyal'. Those not requesting specific brands may still be loyal in purchasing, however; they may simply have difficulties in recall.

In Table 5.2, the data shown in Table 5.1 have been disaggregated into those asking specifically for own-label brands, other named brands and products without specific brands being requested. There were significant differences between the private brand shopper versus the national brand loyal and unknown brand shopper, confirming the hypothesis.

Table 5.2 Brand of item noted as out-of-stock versus action taken (%)

	Store's own label	Other brand	Brand not specified
Purchase same brand different size	8.5	3.4	4.9
Other brand	12.0	10.3	0.1
Other product	12.8	12.0	6.9
Postpone until next visit to store	22.6	8.5	4.9
Decided not to purchase	23.9	7.7	21.6
Decided to search in other store	20.5	66.2	60.8
Total	100.0	100.0	100.0

The proportions searching in other stores are lower, postponing or not purchasing, buying different sizes, other brands or other products are higher. This indicates a higher propensity to stay within the same stores. The differences between 'other' brands and 'unknown' brands are not pronounced.

Does stock-out behaviour influence brand loyalty? The one piece of empirical evidence on this point comes from Charlton and Ehrenberg [2] who performed an experiment with a panel of housewives. One of the customary brands offered to this panel was withdrawn over an extended period. When it returned, there was a shift back to this brand; the interruption apparently had no after-effects.

Does the image of the store change as a result of the stock-out incidence? The third hypothesis states that the effect of stock-outs was to weaken the general image of the store. Both affected and non-affected shoppers were asked to rate the store on seven factors, presumed to be important in shaping store image:

    a product quality
    b service to customers
    c value for money

d convenience
e variety of products available
f product availability
g location

The rating of a particular store could vary not only because of a stock-out, but also because of differing perceptions by respondents in different stores and occupational classes. There were, however, no significant differences in responses by store. Response by social class varied significantly in several instances. The question is whether the stock-out responses differed more significantly from the total response than those of the managerial-occupational class. A positive finding would support the hypothesis. The results are shown in Table 5.3.

Table 5.3 Comparison of significance of store performance perception variables for stock-out and occupational class variables

| Variable | X^2 Confidence level | | Stock-out compared to occupational class |
	Stock-out	Occupational class	
Product quality	0.0001	0.0760	More
Customer service	0.0002	0.0012	More
Value for money	0.0002	0.0713	More
Convenience	0.0389	0.2360	More
Product variety	0.0000	0.0000	Same
Product availability	0.000	0.0322	More
Location	0.1575	0.0511	Less

Comparisons were made by means of x^2 tests; the basis for identifying the highest significance is the lowest probability of a chance error. Recognising that the modal values of all groups studied were unchanged, the differences would be small. Nevertheless, there appear to be attitude differences associated with the stock-out phenomenon, although not necessarily a causal relationship. The stock-out may have caused a shift, but underlying attitudes may have influenced perception of the stock-out. However, images of product quality and value are also affected. There thus appears to be a salient element affecting store image in other areas, resulting directly from the stock-out. As one component of store image, product availability appears then to be influential in shaping a broader image. A store in a similar position should then seek to improve its availability performance as a major step towards improving the total image.

The final question is how a stock-out affects market share. In the short-run, the loss of patronage may not be directly measurable, unless the stock-out problem becomes severe. In the long-term, the effects may be cumulative. In this study it was not possible to measure the direct impact on manufacturers' market share. However, two pieces of evidence from other sources, reported elsewhere [2 and 12], should be considered. In the United States, a local strike against beer distributors left several brands, both local and national, without distribution, while a similar set was untouched. Those able to maintain their distribution increased their shares during the strike. Market share did not return completely to pre-strike positions even two and a half years after the strike was over. Factors other than distribution were also operating: sales effort, promotion and pricing. Two hypotheses were tested: (a) that changes in stock level which affect the probability of stock-outs should influence market share in the same direction in the short-run, and (b) that stock levels would influence market shares in the same direction in the long-run. These hypotheses were tested by two regression equations which measure alternately the short- and long-term influences. Independent variables in both equations were the market shares before and during the strike, and a dummy variable to indicate whether a price change which took place within the industry was applicable to a specific brand or not (the change is denoted by 1, the lack of a change by 0). The dependent variable for the short-term was market share for a four months immediately after the end of the strike; for the long-term, it was market share during the four-month period, two and a half years later. If either equation was consistent with the corresponding hypothesis about signs and magnitudes of coefficients and was statistically significant, it could not be rejected; if one proved to be more statistically significant than the other, that one would be presumed to be dominant. The results are shown in Table 5.4 below.

Table 5.4 Regression analysis: market share and the impact of strike-caused stock-outs

---

1. Short-term:

$$\text{Log MS}_{A1} = 0.060 + 0.731 \text{ Log MS}_B + 0.259 \text{ Log MS}_D - 0.012 \quad P$$
$$\phantom{\text{Log MS}_{A1} = 0.060 +} (1.8) \qquad (14.18) \qquad\qquad (7.3) \qquad\qquad (-.316)$$
$$R^2 = 0.993$$
$$F = 468.9 \quad \text{d.f.} = 1, 6$$

2. Long-term:

$$\text{Log MS}_{A2} = 0.116 + 0.923 \text{ Log MS}_B + 0.093 \text{ Log MS}_D - 0.163 \quad P$$
$$\phantom{\text{Log MS}_{A2} = 0.116 +} (1.03) \qquad (5.24) \qquad\qquad (0.77) \qquad\qquad (-1.26)$$
$$R^2 = 0.918$$
$$F = 31.6 \quad \text{d.f.} = 1, 6$$

Where: MS_{A1} = Market share, post-strike
MS_{A2} = Market share, June, 1974
MS_B = Market share, before strike
MS_D = Market share, during strike
P = Dummy variable: 0 if no price increase/six pack
                  1 if 5¢ price increase

---

t-values appear below coefficients

These results clearly support the effect of a predominantly short-term effect. The explanatory power of the coefficient of determination is higher; the F-statistic is also higher for the short-term equation. The during-strike market share is higher in the short-term equation, and is significant at the 5 per cent level in the short-term but insignificant in the longer-term equation. The pricing term turned out to be insignificant in determining share in this situation; the stock-out effects of the strike were dominant.

Implications

In this study, all four of the hypotheses were affirmed, although the results appear to be specific to the situations involved. The question is now, what direction do they provide for customer service in distribution?

The first two hypotheses were concerned with marketing issues: who notices that products are out-of-stock, and how does consumer behaviour vary by the types of products that were not found? Now that the results are in, how can they help in the management of customer service? First if stock-outs are noticed only by specific market segments, then service at the retail level may be selectively employed. These findings need to be generalised to a larger set of circumstances. If they were found to be more universal, service could then be planned to fit dominant groups of consumers in different store locations. The same levels of service do not need to be applied across the board.

The second finding suggests differing patterns of response to national and private label shopping behaviour. Suppliers of national brand merchandise should try to maintain stocks over wide areas so that if shoppers do not find the product in one store, they may be able to find it easily in the next. Conversely, retailers would be more reluctant to stock national brands if a stock-out causes customers to search in other stores. National brand marketing then requires strong logistic support both to enter markets and to retain market share. Own-label shoppers are less prone to move from one store to another. A stock-out may lead to substitution of another product within the store. Stocking policies by stores might emphasise variety of products as potential substitutes.

The third hypothesis examines the implications of a service failure on the perception of the store. The general image suffers because of a distribution failure, possibly in a very few products. The finding is significant to the store buyer as store image is dependent on the ability of his suppliers or even his own stock management to maintain product availability. This can then be translated back into bargaining pressure on suppliers in turn to provide high levels of service. The fourth is supported by a piece of evidence from another study which indicates that stock-outs lead to at least short-term losses in market position, and possibly even in the long-term.

Potential research in consumer response to out-of-stock situations leads in several directions. One is whether the shopper reporting out-of-stock situations is distinctly different from other shoppers. The evidence here suggests that perception and response predominantly come from a single occupational class. It appears to reflect on the degree of pre-planning of product selections, which is determined by other factors. Other areas are the effects of product availability on other dimensions of store image. There appears to be a saliency stemming from the out-of-stock situation which influences other perceptions. Another is the threshold level of acceptable performance. How high must service be before it is acceptable to consumers?

The entire issue of product availability is open for exploration. In an era in which logisticians and marketers must increasingly recognise physical and financial resource constraints, consumer response to out-of-stock situations must become an important topic.

References

1. Bucklin, Louis P., 'Retail Strategy and the Classification of Consumer Goods,' *Journal of Marketing*, Vol.27 (January 1963), pp.56-58.
2. Charlton, P. and A.S.C. Ehrenberg, 'An Experiment in Brand Choice,' *Journal of Marketing Research*, Vol.XIII (May 1976), pp.156-57.
3. Dommermuth, William P. and Edward V. Cundiff, 'Shopping Goods, Shopping Centers and Selling Strategies,' *Journal of Marketing*, Vol.31 (October 1967, pp.32-36.).
4. Farley, John U., 'Why Does Brand Loyalty Vary Over Products?' *Journal of Market Research*, Vol.1, 1975, p.12.

5. *The Grocer,* November 1, 1975, p.12.

6. 'Growing Problems of Stock-outs Verified by Neilsen Research,' *Progressive Grocer* (November 1968), pp.25-29.

7. Heeler, Roger M., Michael J. Kearney and Bruce J. Mehaffey, 'Modelling Supermarket Product Selection,' *Journal of Marketing Research,* Vol.10 (February 1978), pp.34-37.

8. This model is developed from one described in Monroe, Kent B. and Joseph G. Guiltinan, 'A Path-Analytic Exploration of Retail Patronage Influences,' *Journal of Consumer Research,* Vol.2 (June 1971) pp.19-29.

9. *Neilsen Researcher,* No.3 (1975).

10. 'The Out-of-Stock Study,' *Progressive Grocer,* (October 1968), p.4-5.

11. Schary, Philip B. and Boris W. Becker, 'Distribution and Final Demand: The Influence of Availability,' *Mississippi Valley Journal of Business and Economics,* Vol.8 (Fall 1972), pp.17-20.

12. Schary, Philip B. and Boris W. Becker, 'The Impact of Stock-out on Market Share: Temporal Effects,' *Journal of Business Logistics,* Vol.1 (1978).

13. Shycon, Harvey N. and Christopher Sprague, 'Put a Price Tag on Your Customer Service Levels,' *Harvard Business Review,* Vol.53 (July-August 1975), pp.71-78.

14. Walter, Clyde K. and John B. Grabner, 'Stockout Cost Models: Empirical Tests in a Retail Situation,' *Journal of Marketing,* Vol.39 (July 1975), pp.56-60.

6 Customer service as an operating system

Customer service is conventionally described in terms of performance of the physical distribution system in meeting the explicit demand of customers. Ballou, for example, defines it as 'the quality with which the flow of goods and services are managed' [2,]. Service is portrayed as a set of standards such as the elapsed time between receipt and shipment of orders from a warehouse, the percentage of items demanded which are out-of-stock and similar measures [7] and [8]. Customer service is, however, more than a set of performance standards. It is an interrelationship between physical distribution activities and other functional areas of the company, such as marketing and production. As one observer commented, there are two concepts from physical distribution which cut across the entire corporate organisation; one is the total cost concept, the other is customer service [3].

Customer service is primarily concerned with filling orders. The nature of the process makes customer service into both a processing system and a communications network. The inputs are the flow of orders and coordinating communications. The throughputs are the orders-in-process. The outputs are both the completed transactions and the system performance in meeting the demands of supplier and customers. The communication demands are (1) to perform the order processing operations, (2) to coordinate the activities involved, and ultimately (3) to define the activities and assign them between the customer's and the supplier's organisations.

The customer service system is, however, a link between supplier and customer, rather than a self-contained entity within a single organisation. The purpose of this chapter is to examine the nature of this inter-organisational system as both a communication network and a set of functional operations. Studying the system involves three essential questions:

1   What tasks and elements are specifically included within this system?
2   What determines the structure and characteristics of the customer service system?
3   How can management direct and control the system effectively?

Customer service can be viewed as an application of Ashby's Law of Requisite Variety [1] and [6]. The central concept is that customers create variety in the form of demands on suppliers. Customer service is thus a response by management to the presence of this variety. Controlling variety then becomes the central issue of management of customer service. In order to control variety, the system must adopt specific characteristics of structure and coordination which become unique to the customer service problem.

The initial impetus for this discussion stems from the study of customer service practices of the six manufacturing companies and the analysis of their customer response in Chapters 3 and 4. During the course of the investigation, it became evident that the phenomenon of customer service in distribution included more than performance dimensions alone, but actually involved an interactive system between the supplying and receiving organisations which influenced not only the performance interface but their own organisations and organisational behaviour as well. This chapter is then an initial formulation of the issues of structure and management of customer service systems, intended to provide a basis for further empirical investigation.

Defining the customer service system

Customer service is a process for managing variety. It is specifically concerned with two distinct but interrelated problems: assessing customer demand, and determining the appropriate supplier response. Customers under some conditions will present a wide variation of demands on suppliers, leading to potentially costly response in fulfilling orders. Customers may order in a wide range of order sizes, from individual items shipped as separate packages to large orders with variable numbers of differing items in quantities of truck and rail carload quantities. While some distribution systems will accommodate this range of variety, most will not do it as efficiently as one which is directed towards more specialised activity.

A conceptual model

The fundamental idea of customer service as a variety-managing system is drawn from Ashby's Law of Requisite Variety, which states that 'there must be as many actions available to the system's controller as there are states in the original system' [11]. Customer demands are then seen as a source of variety which is then transmitted through the marketing channel. Each channel member responds to this variety by either matching this variety or by shifting this variety to other members. Matching takes place through customer service which has developed to respond to the variety that is imposed on it.

The flow of and response to variety within a supplier-customer relationship can be seen in Figure 6.1. Variety in the form of product demands flows from the market through an intermediary customer towards a supplier and beyond. Customer and supplier are linked by an inter-organisational system which is identified as customer service. The customer faces a set of variety-generating demands denoted by H(D), imposed by the market. The customer may absorb some of this variety, blocking it from further transmission up the channel by such devices as holding inventory in anticipation of sales. While he may reduce variety, his own order characteristics, or his position in the market may add additional variety. The output of the customer is then a modified variety, H(F), passed on to the customer service system.

Figure 6.1 Variety and the customer service system

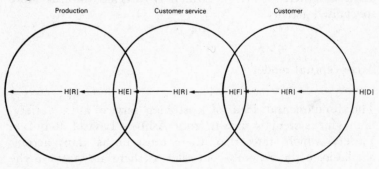

The purpose of the customer service is ostensibly to process orders in order to satisfy customer demands. At the same time it serves as a buffer between the customer's variety and the production area's need for minimal variety, reducing H(F) to H(E). The desirable relationship of system output to input in the transmission of variety may be described by the equation:

$$H(E) \geq H(D)^2 \, Hd(R) - H(R)$$

indicating that the variety transmitted through the organisation H(E) is the sum of the variety encountered initially H(D) plus variety added by the characteristics of the preceding stage, Hd(R) but which is reduced by blocking actions H(R) at each of these stages.

In the succeeding sections, we will examine first some sources of customer-generated variety, describe some strategies to reduce variety within the customer service system, and then proceed to deal specifically with structure and management of the system. In so doing, it is important to remember that variety cannot be reduced without absorbing it somewhere in the system. As Ashby states, 'Only variety can destroy variety' [2].

The demands for customer service

Customers can order products in a variety of ways. The task of customer service is to accommodate this variety in a manner which benefits the customer. Consider a list of causes of hypothetical variations in customer orders:

1 *differences in customer types* — large customers may order in large, fixed quantities; small customers in small and fluctuating volumes. Some customers may plan orders jointly with suppliers; others may suddenly place large orders for immediate delivery

2 *differences in order characteristics* — orders may request unit loads for mechanised materials handling; others may be small quantities from broken lots, delivered as individual shipments

3 *differences in service standards* — customers in highly competitive markets may be able to bargain for precise delivery schedules and inventory holdings by suppliers. In other circumstances, customers may be forced to accept less precise delivery and hold their own stocks.

This is a limited sample of the potentially limitless variety that a customer can impose on a supplier's system. Variety begins with the consumer who shows variation in item selection, quantities and shopping times. Retailers may absorb some of this variety, but through reordering will pass a large share on to the supplier. Retailers may themselves introduce variety through the differences in markets, ordering practices and bargaining power which they bring to the supplier. The service task of the supplier is to accommodate variety by matching it with inventory, rapid delivery, order status information and similar activities.

Variety in a customer service system is a determinant of efficiency. A standardised system will operate with fewer resources because it deals with homogeneous demands and minimises nonstandard communications. Service by definition accommodates variety, but this conflicts directly with the requirements for efficiency. Strategy must then compromise between the amount of variety necessary to absorb into the system and the costs involved.

Conflict may also occur between the dimensions of variety which the system may accept. Order cycle time can be considered as an imposition of variety. Long or erratic order cycle times force customers to absorb variety through larger inventory. Short cycle times require less in resource commitments from these customers. As the order cycle time is decreased, the costs to the supplier of meeting this variety are increased, probably at an exponential rate. However, even for the customer the advent of shorter cycle times present conflicts with other forms of variety such as differences in order size or special handling which create delays and reduce efficiency in the process. From the customer's standpoint, what is gained by the supplier absorbing one form of variety through reduction in order cycle time may be lost through the supplier's inability to absorb other forms of variation.

Variety-absorbing strategies

Customer service is, therefore, a matching process requiring specific judgements about the elements of service and the levels of performance which are important to the customer. Suppliers generally have three options in dealing with this problem: (a) they can absorb variety into their organisations; (b) they can reduce redundant variety by changing their internal systems; (c) they can shift variety, possibly forward to the customer, or backward to other parts of the supplier's organisation.

An extreme example of absorbing variety is the organisation which produces an order to the customer's precise and individual specification. This may require lead time for the order, so that the characteristics of customer orders will be dominant over the time dimension. Managing lead time may require specific variety absorbing strategies, such as maintaining peak workload capacity. Special orders may introduce more production complexity. The result is the creation of a high service but also high-cost system. Further, there must also be a limit to the amount of variety that a system can absorb. This may be evidenced by constraints on the types and numbers of orders and will come about because of the limitations of both tangible resources and management.

A second alternative is to reduce the potential variety within the system. Genuine variety cannot, of course, be reduced but must be matched somewhere in the channel system if it is to be controlled. Redundant variety offers possibilities for potential reduction. This form of variety is found in abundance in most channel systems where assumptions by independent decision-makers create redundant decisions. Examples to reduce this variety include the practice in many customer service programmes to organise customers to order and receive orders on pre-arranged schedules, developing standardised unit modules for uniform materials handling and developing common coding designations.

A third alternative is to shift variety elsewhere, either in the channel or within the supplying organisation. Persuading a customer to hold inventory absorbs fluctuation in demand which might otherwise reach the supplier. Imposition of minimum order size similarly shifts the burden of variety onto the customer. A shift of inventory from a retailer backward to the supplier similarly permits the retailer to shift the service problem away from his own organisation. Finished goods inventory systems in manufacturing which permit back-orders in effect shift variety into production, a practice which may be undesirable from the standpoint of total system costs.

Another form of internal strategy for suppliers is to establish two parallel systems. The first is a standardised system for processing uniform orders. The second would be specifically designed to deal with special orders.

The management of variety

The essential decisions of customer service are those of managing variety. The basic issues are two: (a) whether variety should be absorbed within the system or whether it should be shifted elsewhere; and (b) if it is to be absorbed within the system, where should it be located? These decisions are partly market-related and partly organisational. Accommodation of variety versus efficiency is an important system trade-off, but one of the major determinants of this choice is the interaction which takes place with the market.

The market acts to constrain management choice. A supplier in a competitive market has relatively few options; the nature of market transactions has already dictated his choice. If high service levels are the norm for his market, he must conform. In a more monopolistic market, there are more options because he is in a favourable bargaining position and service is only one of a number of elements which can influence the terms of trading.

The decision to absorb specific types and levels of variety implies shifting the rest back to the customers. Their willingness to accept these conditions reflects the state of the market. At the same time, the process of preselecting only customers with desired variety characteristics defines the market. The market is both an environmental constraint on and an area of influence of management decision.

The specific characteristics of the marketing channel may also influence the amount of variety introduced. The nature of the product and the number of customers may determine the total variety that is released into the system.

The amount of variety that can be absorbed has a finite limit, even if undefined. Gardner and Ashby [5] simulated a general abstract system and found that, as variety was increased, the system suddenly became unstable. This capacity limit can only be specified in growth terms, although managers may sense the extent of the capacity constraint. This may explain, for example, why customer service performance is normally limited to relatively few dimensions such as delivery time, product availability and similar elements. This limit also infers reasons for the emergence of programmed relationships which have as their objectives the reduction of variety within the system.

The location of variety by absorption may also be limited to relatively few functional areas within the organisation. Production efficiency does not lend itself to absorbing variety. Long production runs and materials requirements planning operate best with minimal variety. The task of matching variety, and specifically customer-originated variety tends to fall then on distribution, and more specifically on finished-goods inventory, as a protecting buffer for the production process.

The selection of strategic options leads to implications about the market and service necessary to meet its needs. Shifting variety forward to the customer implies one of three arguments: that total costs are minimised, that customers are selected by their characteristic variety, or that the bargaining power lies with the manufacturer. These may be used in combination. However, if none of these conditions are present, a forward-shifting strategy does not become attractive. The alternative of absorbing variety within the organisation raises the internal costs of operation, requiring that choices be made. The classic examples of the 'logistics trade-off', total cost minimisation which may involve exchanges, for example, between transportation and inventory costs, or increasing service for higher profitability, actually describe choices both about the characteristics and the location of variety within the organisation.

The customer service system

Customer service has distinct characteristics which set it apart from other parts of the supplier's organisation. First, it is an interface between organisations, linking the order acquisition, processing and fulfilment activities of both customer and supplier. By implication, there is at least a minimal consensus on performance expectations. Second, it coordinates the performance of activities because it connects functional areas, which may lead to conflict with the objectives of the two organisations. Third, it implicitly engages the supplier and customer simultaneously at the operating, control and strategic levels of coordination.

The order fulfilment process is in a sense similar to the sales process; both are dyads, boundary-spanning links between formal organisations with disparate goals [10]. Sales and service organisations in practice, however, tend to become almost entirely autonomous of each other. The role of sales is to solicit orders or gain customers. That of customer service is to maintain the flow of orders once established.

The order process involves a prescribed sequence of activities involving both customer and supplier. A typical sequence is shown in Table 6.1. These activities as functional centres also become nodes in a communication network which involves the production of operating documents as well as the coordination needed to ensure the output of completed orders.

Table 6.1 Order-processing tasks in the customer service system

Organisation	Task
Customer	1. Need for item is originated
"	2. Order is placed
Supplier	3. Order is received
"	4. Customer is approved
"	5. Credit is approved
"	6. Order edited
"	7. Order compared to stock on hand
"	8. Order released to warehouse
"	9. Order-picking instructions released
"	10. Order picked and assembled
"	11. Order packed and prepared for shipment
"	12. Order documents prepared
"	13. Transportation documents prepared
"	14. Transportation planning
"	15. Order loaded on vehicle
"	16. Order transported
Customer	17. Order received
"	18. Order placed in stock
"	19. Inventory of customer updated

The operating system as part of the general service system must balance the conflict of service (variety) and costs. This balance determines the structure of the communications network. Efficiency favours complete routinisation with minimal nonstandard communication, which encourages the use of infrequently-changed decision rules. This system can only operate under conditions where variety is constrained within narrow limits.

The goal of establishing routine, however, reduces the potential options for both buyer and seller. Thompson [12] identifies two polar dimensions of the transaction relationship: routinisation and autonomous control. At one extreme is the fully-negotiated transaction when supplier and customer are free to select each other for individual exchange. The other is the programmed relationship of the vertical marketing system in which supplier and customer are closely coupled to produce standardised transactions.

The exclusion of variety from the operating level requires that this variety be shifted, logically to a higher level. This shifted variety includes both special orders and coordination, which would normally be expected at a supervisory level. This then requires a supervisory level to absorb variety, *i.e.* to match variety with variety. This then places demands on the communication network at this level for flexibility to achieve this coordination.

The system must be directed and linked between the customer's and supplier's organisations, requiring negotiation, strategic planning and control. This envisages redesigning the system in response to environmental change and relocating functional activities. These requirements indicate a need for widely-connected networks to absorb new information. The extent of the strategic task in customer service is limited only by the perspective of management. Under adequate recognition and sponsorship, customer service can assume an important role in corporate strategy, with an influence on both customers and internal operations.

The service system involves both hierarchical and lateral structure. Hierarchical refers here to control within organisations; lateral means connections between organisations.

The task differentiation at each level is hierarchical in that routine operations are emphasised at the base and planning becomes more important at the top. These are described in Figure 6.2. These then place different communication requirements on the system. Operation of the order-processing system involves a rigidly-defined communication network. The amount of task variety, however, increases with each level in the hierarchy, increasing the need for more communication channels to deal with the larger amount of variety encountered.

Both customer and supplier have internal hierarchical ordering. In the supplier's organisation, the flow of authority stems from the director of Marketing, Production or Distribution to a customer service manager, and then to the processing units. On the buyer's side, the flow of authority begins with a director of Purchasing or Supply and extends through functional managers to the processing units in the buying organisation. There is, however, no necessary communication between these separate hierarchies.

Figure 6.2 The customer service organisation

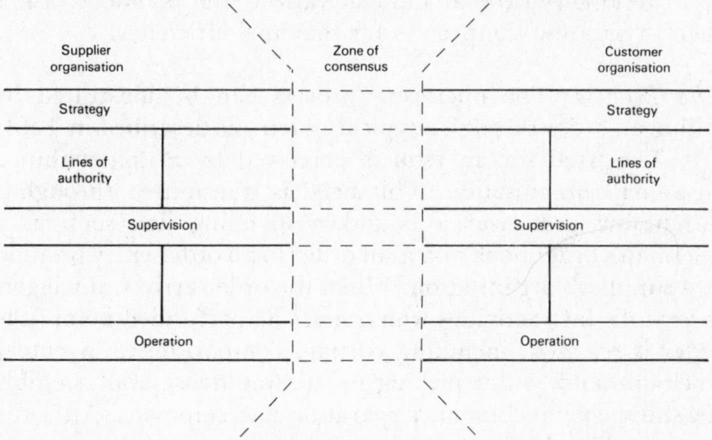

Lateral communications are necessary for the system to operate. The initial basis is the flow of orders and other documentation, originating in the perception of need in the customer's organisation, moving through the supplier's processing operations to result in filled orders and status reporting to the buyer. While the system may possibly operate with minimal consensus, the imperative of service accommodation and efficiency become motivators for strong cooperation, monitoring and coordination of activities. At the highest level is negotiation which determines the nature of this cooperation.

The dilemma of customer service management is how to deal with this combination of hierarchical control and lateral coordination. The former is linked to the organisational boundary, but the latter is clearly trans-organisational, but without commonly-accepted legitimacy of power necessary to secure compliance with coordinative requests.

The operating system

The objective in designing an operating system could be stated as *to fulfil orders at minimum cost, subject to a planned level of variety*. Given the amount of variety, the planner's task is then to organise the process for maximal efficiency.

The Process. The operating process can be illustrated by taking an order through a typical system, as described in Table 6.1. The need for an item is perceived by a unit within a customer's organisation. This need is transmitted through a purchasing unit over a boundary-spanning link such as a salesman's order book or a mail order to an order entry position in a supplier's organisation. When the order arrives, it triggers several distinct activities which must be performed before the order is released, including editing, comparison to inventory stock-on-hand, order picking in the warehouse and assembly for shipment, document preparation and shipment. After the order is shipped, it then re-enters the customer's system as a potentially completed request, being received, compared against the original order, and then moved to stock or to a place of need. At the same time, a signal is released to a record-keeping unit to indicate that the transaction is completed. Acknowledgement of the receipt of the order then closes the physical transaction. In Table 6.1, note that some tasks are in the supplier's domain (steps 3 to 16) and others are in the customer's (steps 1, 2, 17 to 19). However, all are essential to the operation of the system. If there have been no difficulties with the order, there will be no need for further contact on this transaction between the buyer and seller.

The operating links which provide the information and triggering signals can be considered as 'primary' to the system. Behind them are a potential series of coordinating links which organise the work flow and which are then designated as 'secondary'. The operating system is then a communication network which spans two formal organisations: the supplier's and the customer's. The design of an efficient order-processing system requires that communication be limited in order to process orders with minimal disruption. The design objective is to minimise extraneous information flow.

The communication networks. Variety determines the amount of information required, the complexity of the order-processing task and the level of problem-solving required. Complexity is here defined as the number of variables involved, e.g. the order size variation in transportation management. Problem-solving means dealing with ambiguity such as a policy decision about how many back-orders to accumulate before intervening in the system. Galbraith (4) suggests two ways to reduce information: through the use of slack resources and decentralisation. Slack resources are useful in reducing both complexity and ambiguity. The concept of the slack resource is the investment in resources beyond a minimal level in order to reduce the amount of decision and communication involved. Inventory is an example; high stock levels reduce the need for external communications from order processing to stock control, while low stock levels encourage increased communication to stock control and even to production scheduling. The slack resource thus controls the potential complexity of the communication network.

Centralisation. The degree of centralisation also influence the abount of information required within the network. Decentralisation implies that decisions will be made at the level of the functional unit by rules established in advance. Decentralised decision-making is favoured by the development of distributed computer networks which disperse data files throughout the organisation rather than to maintain them solely in a mainframe computer.

System choice is a result of comparing order characteristics and task complexity. Complexity and the volume of communication are closely associated. Decentralisation is favoured where orders involve simple matching against inventory, without permitting back-orders, shipments of uniform size, preferably handled by for-hire carriers (avoiding equipment scheduling). Centralised control is preferable where orders involve individual planning, such as in transportation and production, coupled with rigid delivery-time requirements. Research in social networks indicates that decentralised networks are superior for simple problems but that centralised networks are better for more complex tasks.

The time dimension. Time is an important element in managing variety. Research indicates that centralised social networks are faster for simple problems, decentralised networks are faster for more complex problems. The relevant research, however, deals only with social networks involving human contacts, with limited capacity to deal with problems inter-actively. There comes to mind no corresponding evidence on computer or man-computer systems.

The pressures of service tend to orient order-processing systems towards the reduction of order cycle times. This again emphasises the differences between centralised as opposed to decentralised networks. There appears to be two fundamental choices in the design of order-processing systems: sequential and parallel networks. Parallel networks, as their name implies, involve simultaneous performance of related tasks in the order process and require less total time in theory.

A set of tasks such as those shown in Table 6.1 lead themselves to a sequential path in which one activity follows the other, with each stage triggered by the progress through the preceding stage. This is shown in a simplified form in Figure 6.3a. In contrast is the parallel system in Figure 6.3b with the branching of the order-processing activities. Parallel systems require higher levels of coordination to ensure the completion of all stages on schedule.

In a sequential network, each stage is decentralised, remote from all the others except for those most adjacent and characterised by limited information flow. Each stage may become almost autonomous. Decision-making under these conditions can be more efficient because the complexity of interdependent decisions is reduced. The progress of orders will be slower because of the chain dependency. This system favours processing in which there is a high degree of uncertainty about orders and workload because it demands the least amount of coordination. In effect, variety is managed individually, one stage at a time.

In a parallel network, as in Figure 6.3b, the simultaneous task accomplishment has the advantage of compressing total elapsed time at the cost of potentially higher levels of coordination. As soon as the order is received, it is edited, passed into the computer system to compare against customer, product and inventory files. At the same time, the order is routed both to the warehouse for order assembly and to transportation planning. Branching, however, requires centralised control for coordination. The order entry point thus becomes pivotal, both for divergence of the processing flow and for convergence of information for status enquiries.

In effect, parallel networks shift order cycle time costs in the form of variety onto the supplier. This shifting is feasible only where the inherent variety of the order characteristics are low. Coordination requirements within the supplier's system increase, requiring more communication in order to match the variety introduced by the branching decision.

With irregular demands or other abnormal situations, the variety may exceed the bounds of the system. Coordination requirements would increase. At some point the system may become unstable and cease to function in a predictable manner. At this point the customer may become concerned and add additional communications to establish the status of his orders, as shown in Figure 6.4. Under extreme conditions, the customer may actually attempt to 'manage' his own orders through the supplier's system, confounding the problem even further.

As a protection, it may be important to add a buffering stage, i.e. a 'customer service representative' to buffer the system against unwanted variety by absorbing customer contact and controlling the number of requests permitted into the system. This then serves as a protective filter for the organisation.

Figure 6.3 Order processing network

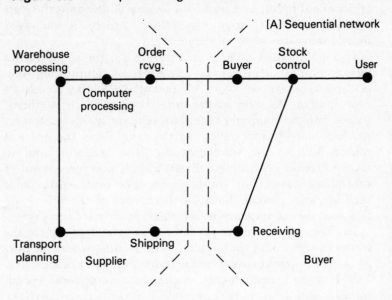

[A] Sequential network

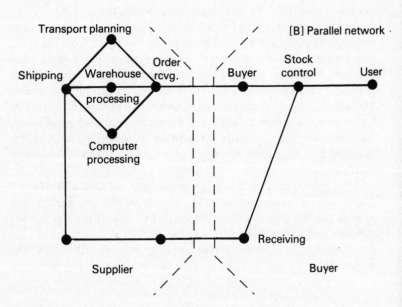

[B] Parallel network

Figure 6.4 Order processing network with inquiries

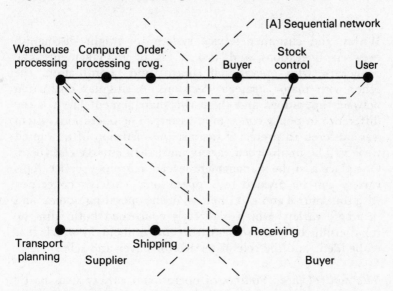

[A] Sequential network

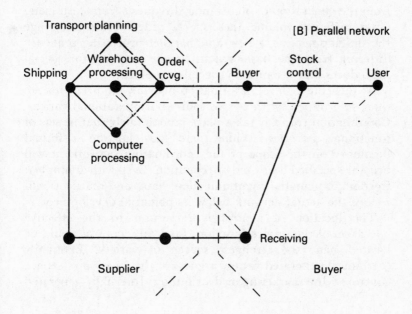

[B] Parallel network

Management systems in customer service

Within the customer service system we might distinguish between operations and two levels of management, one concerned with operational control and coordination, the other with major strategic decisions. A singular distinction between operations and these two management levels is the difference in policy concerning variety. The operations system was buffered to protect it against the intrusion of unwanted variety. The unabsorbed variety must then emerge elsewhere. One place is at the management level of customer service. This variety can be divided into 'operational variety', concerned with the control and coordination of the operating system, and 'strategic variety' which is directly concerned both with the relationship of the system to the environment in which it is embedded, and the role of service for buyer and seller.

The control level. Sources of operational variety stem partly from the management of the operating system, and in part from the generation of non-standard requests from customers. Given sufficient volume, these special orders would encourage the development of a new and parallel processing sequence differing from the basic system by the demand for special procedures and response to special requests.

At this control level, information network requirements are then determined by these two sources of operational variety. Coordination typically takes place among fairly routine sets of functional activities. While there may not be a formal boundary on the scope of the coordinating network, it will become specified over time by repetition. Even with an implied freedom of potential communication, habit and routine would reduce the actual network below its potential development.

The location of control is important to the effective operation of the service function. Logically, control would be located near the strongest source of variety. Externally (customer) generated variety argues for the location of service control within marketing or distribution. Internally-generated variety, such as problems associated with production scheduling, would place it in production.

The strategic level. The level of service strategy deals with a distinctly different set of problems. These are defined by four types of activity:
1 establishing the scope, dimensions, objectives and general direction of the customer service system
2 defining and negotiating service policies and specifically the amount of variety to absorb or to shift elsewhere
3 negotiating with customers to determine the allocation of tasks between organisations
4 designing the internal system and allocating tasks to functional areas within the organisation, decisions which determine the location of variety within the organisation.

Both the nature of strategic service activities and their organisational location are seldom clearly established in advance. The structure of the communications network must therefore be broad in scope in order to respond to a potentially wide variety of strategic decision areas, limited only by the interests and perceptions of upper management. The most highly developed customer service system in our study was controlled by the Director of Distribution. At the same time, this firm was engaged in a unique and significant service project with several major customers to introduce and manage a unitised materials-handling system for more efficient stock replenishment and merchandising at the retail level. Authority and responsibility for the project were being shared between Distribution on the one hand, and a special projects manager from Marketing on the other.

Customer service spans two organisations. Central direction of the customer service system is desirable because it leads to greater efficiency, it permits considering the location of variety within a unified system. Research in communication networks indicates that the strength of the centralised organisation stems not so much from task efficiency as from the increased problem-solving ability of interconnected networks. Under conditions of rapid environmental change, systems respond most effectively by a unified response. The problem is complicated, however, by the need to preserve organisational boundaries.

Boundary-spanning cooperation becomes difficult to manage at upper levels of the service system. Recalling Figure 6.2, the two parallel hierarchical structures present an obstacle to integrated control. Direct control is necessary, but is possible only within the bounds of a single organisation. When control is extended to an inter-organisational process, control becomes indirect and limited to lateral coordination and persuasion.

Management of customer service

Variety has been viewed as a determinant of structure. Even with the ability to predict the organisational characteristics, the problem still remains about how to manage customer service as variety within a boundary-spanning system. The relationships have already been established by the common problems of information and the flow of goods. The most pressing aspect of customer service is the need for coordination where lines of authority cannot be directly established.

The central issue is control. The locus of this control is presumed to lie with the strongest interest in the service process, the supply side of the transaction. While there are problems of inter-functional cooperation, even diverse functional areas operate under a single hierarchical authority. A more difficult area is that dealing with coordination between organisations. There appear to be three distinct constraining factors:

1 boundaries are insuperable limits to direct authority, reporting relationships, lines of command and organisational rewards stop at the boundary

2 perceptions of supplier service will vary not only among customers but also by the role positions of individuals within the customer's organisation. A manager within a customer's organisation perceives critical dimensions in relation to his own

tasks, evaluating suppliers according to their ability to perform on these dimensions
3   organisations have differing objectives which may conflict, affecting the success of service negotiation. Only suppliers are concerned with the direct costs of service unless it affects prices. Customers are concerned with indirect costs. Both will tend to suboptimise. Moreover, the objectives of overall system management are presumed to be a balance of costs and service through decision to absorb and locate variety within the organisation. These considerations may be remote from the actual science of the operating decision

Where direct control is not possible, the only option is to develop lateral coordination. This leads to two alternative strategies. The first is aggregative but essentially non-interactive, leaving each organisation independent and without normal system connections. Service is regarded as a collective marketing problem, in which market standards are administered to all customers. The alternative is to consider major customers as unique markets in themselves. This involves intensive investigation of needs of these customers, leading to higher levels of system interaction. The problem of variety is then handled on an individual customer basis, a position which might be modified to deal with identifiable market segments, which have variety-generating character-istics in common.

The management of customer service as variety is then a marketing dialogue. The customer's organisational needs and perceptions are identified. The supplier then responds with specific system elements to improve the performance of the combined customer-supplier system. This approach would focus on these areas: the present operating system, needs and perceptions.
1   *The customer's operating system:* intensive study of the customer should reveal not only the procedure involved in processing orders but also sources of variety generation which may influence system performance.
2   *Customer needs:* service is a bargaining relationship in which the customer may be unable to identify specifically his

own needs for service, other than for general standards of performance. This part of the study should attempt to identify which elements of variety are necessary for the customer to absorb, and which characteristics can be most efficiently passed back to the supplier.

3 *Customer perceptions:* the impressions of specific supplier performance should be conditioned by the types of variety encountered, both as inherent in the task environment of the individual and the variety imposed by the supplier.

Being perceptual, these evaluations may be based on subjective cues, which should be identified and modified to provide more objectivity. A continuing problem in perception is the effect of responding to these perceptions by creating excessive, even redundant variety. A systemic view may suggest that it is more efficient to change a perception than to create redundant variety.

The results should guide a specific organisational response which in effect becomes a marketing strategy for customer service, focused on specific organisations. A marketing response in customer service would endeavour to attach needs, fit potential service dimensions into the customer's order-processing system and managing perceptions to make them more consistent with the objectives of an inter-organisational system. Elements as examples of this type of strategy would include modification of order-processing decision rules to accommodate the specific order patterns of individual customers, developing common documentation and coding systems, and developing data-retrieval systems for the customer which would provide better data on system and supplier performance. All of these are in practice today. In the context of a customer service system, they should be linked to achieve common system objectives.

Concluding remarks

Customer service as a set of performance standards is an unsatisfying concept. Customer service is foremost a process by which orders are filled. The nature of the process links two organisations together through the functional activities involved. As a process, it takes on the characteristics of an inter-organisational system linking supplier and customer together. The essential characteristic of the system is the management of variety. Customer service management involves decisions about whether to absorb variety or to shift it elsewhere. With absorption, there is a decision about how and where to manage it within the organisation. Variety then determines the structure and the requirements for inter-organisational coordination.

Customer service is a link in a chain between buyer and seller. It is also one of a series of links between stages in a marketing channel. It binds the supplier to a customer who in turn is connected to another buyer. In a context in which marketing is concerned about minimising the costs of the marketing channel as an integral unit, customer service becomes the mechanism by which costs are shifted within the channel.

In another sense, customer service is more than an order-processing activity. It is a precursor of other inter-organisational systems in which the bond is cooperative effort to achieve common goals. Development of these inter-organisational systems is itself a process in which all organisations have a stake.

References

1. Ashby, W. Ross. *An Introduction to Cybernetics,* (London: Chapman and Hall, 1956).

2. Ballou, Ronald H. *Basic Business Logistics,* (Englewood Cliffs, N.J: Prentice-Hall, Inc., 1978), p.62.

3. Beier, Frederick J. 'The Life Cycle of Logistics Departments', *International Journal of Physical Distribution,* Vol.3, (Summer 1973), p.312.

4. Galbraith, Jay. *Organizational Design,* (Reading, Mass: Addison-Wesley Publishing Company, 1977), Chapter 3.

5. Gardner, M.R., and W.R. Ashby, 'Connectance of Large Dynamic-Cybernetic Systems: Critical Values for Stability,' *Nature,* Vol.228 (1970), p.784.

6. Gattorna, J.L. *The Effects of Innovation of Channels of Distribution,* (Cranfield, England: Unpublished doctoral dissertation, 1978) Chapter 3.

7. Heskett, J.L. 'Controlling Customer Service,' *International Journal of Physical Distribution,* Vol.2 (June 1971), pp.141-5.

8. LaLonde, Bernard J. and Paul H. Zinszer. *Customer Service: Meaning and Measurement* (Chicago: National Council of Physical Distribution Management, 1976).

9. Lindzey, Gardner and Leslie Aronson. *Handbook for Social Psychology Vol.IV, Second Edition,* (Reading, Mass: Addison-Wesley Publishing Company, 1969), pp.150-155.

10. Pruden, Henry and Richard M. Reese, 'Interorganization. Role-Set Relations and the Performance and Satisfaction of Industrial Salesmen,' *Administrative Science Quarterly,* Vol. 17 (December 1972), pp.601-609.

11. Schoderbek, P.P., A.G. Kefalas and C.G. Schoderbek, *Management Systems: Conceptual Considerations* (Dallas, Texas: Business Publications, Inc., 1975), p.348.

12. Thompson, James L., 'Organizations and Output Transactions,' *American Journal of Sociology,* Vol.68 (1962), pp.302-324.

7 Strategy in customer service

Strategy, someone once said, is the act of developing plans today to establish future positions tomorrow. This chapter is concerned with the question: What types of planning should be undertaken in customer service which will result in improved market positions within a specified time-period? The process of strategy in a service context involves selecting from among options which will set a direction for future development of the service system. The potential number of options and combinations of options can be immense, but the number of feasible courses of action is limited by the constraints of resources, market forces and the objectives which are possible to attain. The procedural process of developing a customer service strategy is straightforward. Hutchinson and Stolle [5], for example, suggest that there are six major steps:

1 defining the service options
2 determining market preferences
3 selecting elements and synthesising a service 'package'
4 developing a programme to 'sell' customer service
5 performing a market test
6 establishing performance controls.

In this view of customer service, the process begins by considering a now-conventional list of service dimensions: order cycle time and its components, delivery time and its variations, inventory service performance, minimum order, treatment of special orders, order status information and other aspects of the direct fulfilment process. Determining market preferences can be accomplished through research into customer needs and perceptions, following techniques of experimentation, surveys and individual case investigations. Options are then selected by the degree to which the most promising elements contribute to organisational objectives. The selected options must then be integrated into a 'package' of alternatives which meet both an external standard of customer acceptance and internal standards of feasibiity, coherence and profitability. The final steps are to market the package as a product to customers utilising steps for testing the product in the marketplace, promoting it, and establishing standards for evaluation.

In concept, this process is simple, although it may have some difficulties in application. However, the major problem is that it confines strategic thinking to a limited set of options, bound to the present configuration of the physical distribution system. Service is one component of a broader set of channel relationships in which intermediaries, functions and service become ultimately determined by market forces and pressures for system efficiency. Service strategy ultimately implies performance at the point of final use, however far that may be from the point of decisions. In this broad strategic context, the necessity for global system performance creates the necessity to examine new inter-organisational systems, more complex and pervasive in influence than the service relationships in operation today.

In this chapter, we wish to focus specifically on the issues of service strategy. The discussion will proceed from the unique characteristics of service strategies, through a review of the market environment affecting service decisions, establishment of objectives, and setting future courses of action to the implementation of strategy in dealing with organsations. The basic thread is that customer service should be considered broadly, and that only from this perspective can service policies develop to meet the underlying needs that service is intended to fulfil.

Characteristics of the customer service decision

What is involved in customer service which sets it apart from other decision areas of the firm? What do they indicate for future strategies? From the findings of the study and from other discussion of the topic, there appear to be at least six distinct areas of significant difference:

Customer service is a set of interface activities between organisations. As such, it is part of a larger system for the movement of products from supplier to the final customer. Each interface in the system links a buyer and a seller. The combined system is then larger than the decision boundaries of any individual firm. Strategic decisions must incorporate steps to influence and respond to other system members. Parallel to the sales organisation, customer service involves frequent functional contact with members of the customer's organisation. A management objective is to facilitate the flow of coordinating communications to enable the physical movement of goods to take place without impediment.

Customer service is part of the total market offering of the firm. Service influences demand because of the differences in quality of performance by different suppliers. It can be evaluated by buyers in comparison with other factors which influence the sale. It is interrelated with other elements in the marketing mix, such as pricing, promotion, product support and credit, and can be used in substitution. Service is however intangible and difficult to visualise without resort to abstract statistical measures. This requires agreement between buyer and seller on the selection and relative importance of specific elements of service.

Customer service is directly concerned with relationships with market intermediary firms, rather than the final customer. Exceptions can obviously be found, but the majority of interface relationships in consumer goods other than mail order are concerned with intermediary organisations. This requires specific marketing approaches to deal with the problems of these customers, who are motivated by considerations different from those of their customers. In general, demands for service become reflections of power in the channel. Service may influence the final market only indirectly through its influence on the reseller.

Service is perceived asymetrically; good service is expected as a normal concomitant of business relationships; weak service becomes a highly visible negative signal. Service is invisible in the sense that it does not evoke positive response when it exceeds threshold levels of acceptability. Bad service, however, stands out through perceptions of individual incidents. Evaluation of service in the absence of unbiased and systematic information collection becomes highly subjective. Strategy must therefore include provision to reduce subjective aspects of service performance.

Service failures have different consequences in the long-run as opposed to the short-run. Individual short-run failures may not carry long-term consequences. Stock-outs may only result in the loss of single transactions or individual accounts. In the long-run, sustained failure may create more permanent effects, such as the loss of market share, and the deterioration of buyer-seller relationships with a loss of future revenue streams.

Service strategies take on distinctly different characteristics between the short- and the long-run. Short-term strategies deal with a restricted set of dimensions and opportunities for service. In the long-run, there are opportunities to examine the service relationship with fewer restrictions because institutions can be redefined and the effects of market and technological pressures can be taken directly into account.

The result of these characteristics is that policy decisions do not ordinarily result in immediate response, but have effects extending over a considerable time-period. Part of the reason is the subjective nature of evaluation of service. Without objective references, customers may not be able to respond to subtle changes in the system.

The integrative nature of customer service also delays response. Within the supplier firm, customer service is involved with a broad set of functional activities extending across the organisation. In its boundary-spanning role, it links the systems of customer and supplier together. Furthermore, in the full context of the customer service role, it becomes coextensive with the marketing channel, a series of individual interfaces extending from sources of material and components to the final customer.

The danger in strategic choices in customer service is that either they become limited to the point of inefficient suboptimisation, or they embrace so much of the larger system as to become ineffective. The strategic dilemma is then one of either too much or too little.

Setting for strategy

Customer service decisions are made in the context of a larger marketing strategy. Marketing deals with exchange relationships with customers. Customer service is one interface within this relationship. The role of customer service in marketing is to maintain a bond with a customer through servicing of orders, a bond that was initially established by the sales force. In this role, customer service provides a basis for continued customer contact to coordinate orders and adjust service to meet market requirements. Service is therefore only one of several elements encompassed within a marketing strategy intended to influence the demand for the products of the firm.

Marketing strategy utilises a set of potential variables identified as the marketing mix. These variables can normally be classified under the headings of product, promotion, pricing and distribution. In both consumer goods and industrial marketing, these variables can be directed to either the intermediate or the final user of the product. However, the choice of variables and their applications will be distinctly different for the two.

The role of customer service in the marketing mix has not been well-defined in the marketing literature. The assumption is normally made that service will be adequate to enable other variables such as promotion, product, pricing and the exchange relationships of distribution to operate without a lack of products to sell. Service has thus been implicitly excluded from strategy formulation.

When service is explicitly utilised, it is directed to the intermediate buyer, to interact with other aspects of channel operation. Service in effect can be evaluated in a trade-off with other elements specifically directed to the trade. Ease of ordering and prompt delivery can in some occasions be substituted for promotion or pricing elements. Under specific conditions, service can thus become integrated into the marketing mix.

There are two dominant elements which define the role of customer service in marketing strategy. One is market share; the other is the product life cycle. Market share, the position of the firm within its market, is important in two respects. First, in competition, market structure determines the degree of rivalry of competitors. Rivalries tend to be high where product differentiation is low, and products take on the characteristics of commodities with interdependent pricing. Under these conditions, customer service becomes an important determinant of sales. The polar opposite, monopoly, involves products without ready substitutes, a low degree of competitive interdependence and lessened importance for customer service in determining sales. The majority of products tend to fall between these extreme positions. Service thus plays important but specifically-defined roles within each product market.

The second aspect of market share is concerned with vertical relationships within the marketing channel, and specifically dominance in the bargaining relationship. This depends in part on market power, reflected in the alternatives open to buyers and sellers. Dominant sellers can impose their service levels on weaker buyers. Conversely, dominant buyers can force sellers to provide higher levels of service. Thus, service becomes a result of bargaining within a larger set of channel relationships.

The point where service becomes an important element in marketing strategy is determined by product life cycle. This concept defines the sale pattern of products by stages: introduction, growth, saturation and decline, based on the profile of sales volume. It has useful implications for the development of marketing strategy and more specifically here for distribution service. One discussion by Mickwitz [4], for example, indicates that the market response to distribution service and hence its priority in marketing strategy tends to be low until saturation is reached. As the competitive advantage of the product diminishes, and buyers become willing to substitute, distribution becomes more important as a factor in marketing strategy. Furthermore the importance of service is emphasised by the fact that most products lie in the mature stage of their development. However, as revenues decline, pressures are generated to reduce costs, ultimately leading to decisions about when the product should be dropped from the line.

There are financial implications from both market share and product life cycle which are combined in an analytical framework proposed by the Boston Consulting Group [3]. Products are classified according to whether they have high or low growth rates or large or small shares of the market. This produces four product classifications:

1 *'Stars'* — products with high growth rates and high market share. These are the most important products in the product portfolio as they are establishing the company's market position for the future. The service role of distribution with 'stars' is one of support, to ensure product availability as sales increase. Forecasting and inventory investment become important elements.

2 *'Question Marks'* — products with high growth rates but

smaller shares as yet. Their success in the market will depend on demand-generating marketing variables. The service role of distribution is again to support sales and to improve market penetration.

3 *'Cash Cows'* — products with large shares but with little growth. This is analogous to the mature stage of the product life cycle. These products are important in generating cash flow to support the development of future 'stars'. There is little requirement for investment except to maintain the product in the market. The role of service becomes very important to this stage, as substitutability of products becomes more significant. Interruptions of service may lead to deterioration of market positions.

4 *'Dogs'* — products with low growth and low shares. These are candidates to be dropped from the line. Cost considerations including distribution costs become important in the decision. There may be strong arguments for reducing distribution service, e.g. service levels, as a way of improving cash flow.

Setting objectives for a customer service strategy

Marketing strategists would set objectives by comparing the revenues generated from marketing programmes to their related expenditures. The strategy which earns the highest profit then becomes the one that is selected. This relationship is described in Figure 7.1 below. For low levels of expenditure, low levels of response are expected. As outlays increase, the response should increase at a faster rate over a critical range. Finally, at higher levels of expenditure, there may be only a small increase in response. The level of expenditure is determined by the maximum positive difference between revenues from market response and the costs involved. Strategies are selected by comparing the result of these revenue and cost differences.

Figure 7.1

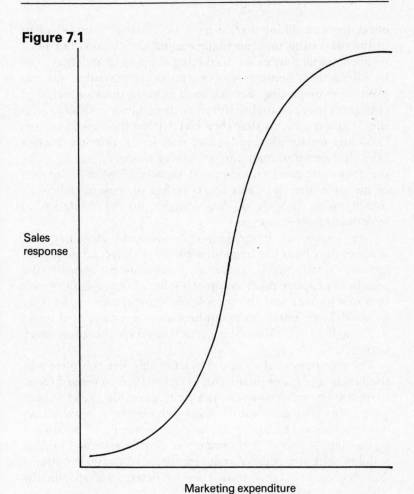

Sales
response

Marketing expenditure

The difficulties in applying this concept directly to customer
service are considerable. A response function implies a
sensitivity by the market to small changes in expenditures. The
asymmetric response by the market to different levels in service
may make this implication weaker than it should be. There
may be substantial lags both in achieving performance and

obtaining a matching market response. Service, as one element in the marketing mix, normally cannot stand alone but must be accompanied by other marketing support. There may thus be interactions between service and other variables, such as promotion or pricing. Service itself is multi-dimensional, and customers may respond to different dimensions in dealing with the unique problems that they face within their own systems. Customer service also tends to be reactive. It does not initiate sales, but serves to maintain or enlarge shares of purchases by previously acquired customers. It therefore becomes difficult to measure directly. Thus for a variety of reasons the profit maximisation models do not provide strong guidance to selecting service strategies.

The degree of interdependence between customer and supplier may limit the freedom available to select strategies. In channel relationships, there is a continuum between the completely captive relationship of a seller or buyer dealing with only one partner and the completely autonomous relationship in which large number of suppliers and customers deal freely with each other. Most service relationships lie somewhere between.

The initiative in the captive relationship lies completely in the hands of the dominant party. Other than to reduce costs, there are few service options normally available to the weaker party. In contrast, autonomous relationships open many service options, although resource commitment may be limited by the short tenure of the transaction. Customer service implies stability, but at a price of reduced choice of strategic options. The degree of balance must then be determined specifically within the market relationship.

Because the underlying goals of customer service cannot be related directly to specific service actions, objectives must be established using proxy measures. These are normally indicators of service performance such as order cycle time and product availability, comparing operations against a predetermined measure, which by assumption and investigation are believed to be related to underlying goals of customer preference and hence market share and profit.

Customer preferences, however, are shaped by the asymmetry of service perceptions, that good service is 'invisible' and bad service is influential. Tangible objectives should then focus on the reduction of negative perceptions. The underlying objective, at least in the short-run, appears to be reduction of 'transactional resistance', the amount of customer effort and resources required to maintain his supply.

The difference between short- and long-term goals now becomes apparent. Short-term objectives should be directed to the reduction of friction within the system to the customer, reducing the problems of coordination and reordering to minimal levels. In the long-run, service is an effort to deal with the system, to reduce system costs, possibly through changes in system design. While short-run objectives may leave the system undisturbed, long-run objectives may substantially alter the relationship between organisations.

All objectives, both short- and long-term, should be measurable, so that progress towards fulfilling a strategy can be established. Internal performance measures have the advantage of measurability. Customer satisfaction can also be measured, although with less accuracy. Long-run objectives appear to have this characteristic in theory, such as the reduction in total system costs, although in actual practice the problem of data collection and the confounding impact of multiple influences make the problem more difficult.

Options in a customer service strategy

The purpose of identifying potential options is to provide a sense of direction for particular aspects of strategy. A complete catalogue of options would be impossible, given the complexity of the customer service problem. The value of categorising options is that it allows analysis to take place within a narrower focus.

For strategic options in customer service, there appear to be two general dimensions: those relating to either external or internal relations and short- and long-term horizons. Customer service should be externally oriented, and some strategies are concerned with interaction with customers. Other options involve improvement of the service process itself and are thus primarily internal. In addition, a general category is needed to relate internal actions to outside forces.

The division between short-term and long-term is arbitrary, normally depending on the time frame for implementation and response. A short-term strategic option is restrictive; roles are established, the environmental influences of the market, the formal organisation and technology are fixed. By contrast, the long-term by definition allows for the possibility of change in any one or several of these dimensions. Market changes, for example, may force a careful re-evaluation of the entire relationship with customers leading to reorganisation of the entire process of fulfilling orders. Strategic options then take on the power to alter the internal organisations of both buyers and sellers. This framework and some examples of options within each of these categories is shown in Table 7.1. One dimension is the division among internal, external and general strategies which combine both internal and external aspects. The other dimension is the time horizon in which the decision is made.

Table 7.1 Framework for customer service strategy

Time horizon	General	Internal	External
Short-term	Develop customer service package	Improve customer service system	Establish permanent links with customer over service
Long-term	Redesign logistics system	Redesign computer-based order-fulfilment system	Establish functional inter-organisational systems

Options are not mutually exclusive. A strategy can provide a mixture of general, internal and external options. It can move through a series of short-term solutions to problems towards a long-term solution. A strategy is thus a set of options encompassing several dimensions, but bound together by an overriding objective which management wishes to achieve. Before attempting to define general strategies, however, some of the options potentially available should be examined.

General strategy options involve both external and internal elements. Essentially, they constitute the main thrust but not the complete set of possibilities in service strategy. Short-term general strategies follow the Hutchinson and Stolle procedure outlined at the beginning of the chapter.

In the short-run, all environmental variables are assumed to be unchanging. Further, no changes are anticipated in organisational arrangement. The only elements of the system which can be changed are those which directly and immediately involve the customer, i.e. delivery, stock availability and related elements. Even to consider these as an integrated unit, however, represents a major change in perspective for many organisations for it forces consideration of service as a product in itself.

In the long-run, service must respond to changes both in the requirements of the market place and developments in organisational structure. At that point, customer service should be the focal point of strategy which considers both the interface and the underlying determinants: channel structure, organisation and the need for functional shifts between separate organisations. The objective of this strategy must be to minimise total channel system costs and improve the level of service through management of change and the development of decision rules to operate the system as an integral unit. Strategy must, therefore, consider not only the contemporary market place, but also its future direction. Establishing the future then becomes a basis for evaluating the potential impact of strategic choices.

Parallel to these general alternatives are a set of internal options. Short-run options are directed towards improvement in the processing of orders. Short-run strategies may involve improvements in coordination among functional areas, improvements in the order-fulfilment communication network and the development of effective monitoring systems to establish firm control over internal processes.

Long-run internal options appear to be strongly influenced by the direction of computer technology. Customer service relies heavily on information technology and its capabilities. The long-run influence, however, is more than technological. Changes in computer systems architecture from central mainframe systems towards distributed data-processing networks tend to decentralise the information base of the organisation. As the information system is thus reordered, so also will be the internal organisation. The tendency to decentralise will be further reinforced by more interactive relationships to external systems, as exemplified by proposals for widespread computer-to-computer reordering, direct customer interrogation about order status, and common coding.

There is another area where external relationships may influence internal systems: materials handling. Pressures on system costs are encouraging the development of standardised modules. Customer service may require accommodation to the need to reduce multi-stage processing costs through acceptance of unit loads which are not optimal from the standpoint of individual firms.

These external influences are subject to specific strategy options. In the short-run, the strategic emphasis is on devices to coordinate relationships between suppliers and customers. This might include more intensive study of customer needs and establishment of more formalised communication networks to transmit performance data, operating information and new preference requests. Because customer perceptions are subject to organisational distortion, a strategic option might include programmes to change these perceptions through providing customers with the means to monitor service or improving the customer's internal communications about service.

The long-run external options involve system relationships,

the scope of which it becomes difficult to visualise today. The use of customer service as a marketing tool is one step in this direction. Further development will require the development of supra-organisational entities oriented around the development of integral channel systems. Under these conditions organisational boundaries will become less relevant.

Throughout this discussion is an emphasis on an interim organisational objective; customer service is an integral part and should be planned as a component of a strategy in which the organisation offers both the traditional 'tangible' product and the intangible service 'products'. Both are tandem outputs of the system. The traditional product is the normal object of the buyer-seller transaction. The service product provides the underlying vehicle in which repeated transactions are possible. The achievement of this perspective, however, requires a reorientation towards the role and value of service in the market.

Elements of a customer service strategy

Strategy looks to the future. The task for developing customer service strategy must recognise the nature of the decision involved, its systemic relationships, the difficulties in perception of change, its role within a larger bargaining framework and the differences in orientation between the short- and the long-run. The role possibilities for customer service are limited by market considerations. Service is one element in the marketing mix, directed towards intermediaries in a strategy which places its major emphasis on the end user. Service is one of several elements which must be used interactively. The importance of service is determined in large measure by the state of the product life cycle, being more important at product maturity than at the stages which precede it. Service is affected by the position of the firm in the market. Large shares provide bargaining power with customers. Small shares indicate a need to respond more to customer service requirements. Service strategies thus appear to be bounded in many directions.

Marketing strategies can be divided by objectives into growth, retention and withdrawal strategies. Growth is an anomolous position for customer service. Service does not ordinarily dominate in growth strategies. Growth through the dominant use of service depends on specific conditions in the market, where an aggressive firm can identify important service voids in the market. It depends on the ability to respond with speed, to gain a competitive edge and seek ways to hold it. It also depends on competitors who are either weak or slow to respond.

Short-run strategies for growth require putting the organisational house in order, to minimise transactional resistance. This, however, may not be enough. It may require a two-pronged attack to identify the real needs of the market, coupled with a programme to make the customer aware of good service when it arrives. A strategy such as this will probably not make major incremental gains at any one time. There are many cases however where strategies such as this have paid off in the steady erosion of competitors' positions.

A major chain of consumer hardware dealers was created through a franchising effort by the wholesaler. Individual stores are free to purchase wherever they wish, subject to a minimum amount purchased through the wholesaler. However, the wholesaler has encouraged stores to purchase electronic order-entry equipment and to arrange stock on the shelf so that orders can be entered directly into the computer in pre-established sequence. The result has been an improvement in order cycle time leading to a shift in patronage towards this wholesaler.

A food supplier to the fast-food restaurant trade had located a warehouse close to competitor's producing area. Bad weather closed down access between the competitor and his major accounts. The new supplier, however, was able to respond almost immediately. The result was a permanent shift in market share in what is normally a commodity product.

In automobile parts, in both England and the United States,

trade journals have reported supplier-based programmes to manage inventories of major customers on the suppliers' computers. Customers report their sales by item in periodic schedules, and the supplier replenishes their stocks, taking this function over from the customer.

In all these cases, customers have not only responded to service improvements through increased sales, suppliers have created systems which are difficult for competitors to emulate successfully. Once a relationship is established, successful systems management can be instrumental in maintaining it.

Short-term moves should be components of long-term strategies designed to establish permanent positions in the market. Strategies can be visualised as a series of short-term steps designed to create long-term system development. They should result in buyer-seller relationships which involve long-term mutual task obligations, which involve interdependent behaviour by both parties. Further, they should be selected with barriers of cost or organisational commitment which can inhibit the influence of competitors who might try to imitate the relationship.

Cost-shifting through functions performed by the supplier for the buyer are strong moves in this direction. The cage pallets cited before were instigated by a major retailer who was entering the market [1]. Cages were adopted tentatively by a large number of major suppliers. They were soon adopted by other retailers; in the meantime the new entrant had carved out a major share of the market, by capitalising on the efficiencies inherent in the cage system.

Maintenance of markets is a more recognisable position than acquisition of market share for service in marketing strategy. In its customer retention role at the maturity stage of the product life cycle, service plays an important role. Markets are seldom static over a long period of time. If service falters, buyers have many options: to select from alternative sources, to de-emphasise the supplier's product and to create new brands. The fundamental objective of service policies is to avoid introduction of inventory disturbances into the system. Once a product is stocked out at a retail level, the consumer may decide on one of several alternatives, one of which is not to buy the supplier's product again.

The options employed may appear to be similar to that of the growth situation, but the collective thrust is different. The one addition is a concern with costs. At this point, both supplier and customer should be concerned with profit margins on individual products. Service strategies are then a balance between attributes such as product availability and delivery and the costs of service to bring the product to the point of final use. Whereas growth strategy tends to be opportunistic, maintenance strategies should be more concerned with long-term system development.

Service strategies are part of a bargaining process. The results should depend on the collective assemblage of marketing elements that the seller can offer, including those factors of uniqueness which differentiate his product. The result of bargaining, however, should be a combined product package: the physical product as the object of the process and the service package which reduces the cost of bringing it to market.

Organisation and the implementation of service strategy

Customer service strategies are inter-organisational in nature. They have the power to alter and potentially to disrupt the operations of the organisations of both the supplier and customer. Therefore, any change introduced though a service strategy will be resisted unless there are strong motivating reasons for its implementation. This motivation may stem from external pressure from competition, or possibly as a result of increased technological possibilities in transportation, materials handling or processing of information. It may be internally motivated, such as the pressures generated by the need to reduce costs. Against this motivation are forces of organisational resistance which may directly oppose change for its own sake, or which may exhibit outward signs of acceptance but which will subvert major changes into smaller issues to limit the degree to which the changes induced by the new service can be manifested.

The major problem in implementing new service strategies does not appear to be technological but organisational. The behaviour of bureaucratic organisations becomes a barrier to implementation whihc must be understood and recognised within a service strategy if that strategy is to be accpted. Cyert and March studied the decision-making processes of the firm, and have described four major concepts as building blocks of this behaviour [2].

1   quasi-resolution of conflict
2   uncertainty avoidance
3   problemistic search
4   organisational learning

How can these concepts contribute to the implementation of service strategies?

Taking the first, the quasi-resolution of conflict recognises that conflict is inherent in relationships both within and between organisations and their sub-units. It begins with differences in goals and objectives,˙ but is also clearly evident in specific operating practices, organisational value-sets and general management styles. In the service setting, two organisations operating independently recognise a common purpose in cooperation. The individual organisational goals, such as standards of profitability or market position, become constraints within which bargaining may take place. The introduction of a potential service strategy is involved with conflict because one party seeks to alter the behaviour of the other party. The intended result is a shift in behaviour leading to greater interdependency and closer market relationships. Conflict under these conditions is not only inevitable but may even increase to the point that the buying organisation may resist the change.

Several approaches have been suggested to reduce inter-organisational conflict. One is defined as local rationality. Organisations are divisible into functional sub-units. If the scale of the potential change is matched to the authority span of the units themselves, it may be possible to resolve conflict at an operating level. Service improvements can be recognised an dealt with more effectively if they are categorised as inventory, management, expediting procedures, delivery, and other functional dimensions with which the customer can deal as separate issues.

A second way to reduce conflict is through joint search, i.e. negotiation for acceptable decision rules. What is acceptable to both sides may not be optimal from the standpoint of the system as a whole, but a search for the 'best' procedure may be implausible. The objective is then to find a solution which may provide less than global optimality, but which can be made to work by both parties. The degree to which decisions have been fragmented and negotiated may accentuate the discrepancy between optimality and acceptability, leaving a situation in which the potential is not fully utilised. This, however, may provide negotiating room for local adjustment.

A third approach to conflict reduction has been to pursue goals in sequence rather than simultaneously. This may have the advantage of avoiding direct goal conflict because only one goal is considered at a time. As a strategy, a series of objectives can be introduced over time, to permit both organisations to adapt to the new system gradually, rather than to introduce new, abrupt and potentially disruptive change at one point in time.

The second building-block concept is uncertainty avoidance. Members of bureaucratic organisations prefer to avoid uncertainty. Any new innovation introduces questions, not only about performance but also about intraorganisational relationships. A major thrust of the implementation of service strategy should seek to reduce uncertainty. Two ways in which this can be done are through wide participation by all parties, and by rapid response to feedback. Service strategies change the decision rules under which customers operate. Those who are thus affected need to participate in the decision. The danger to the supplier is that the system becomes a basis for further extending the objectives. Problem-solving tends to concentrate in areas of success, and avoids areas of failure.

Service strategies should, therefore, recognise a dynamic effect on the inter-organisational relationship, that it may be as well to start with limited objectives in order to permit a positive reaction to immediate system performance and to use this as a building block to further objectives. This is diametrically opposed to a more formalistic approach which defines the strategy first and then seeks to implement it.

Application

What lessons can be applied to the implementation of strategy in the inter-organisational area of customer service? First, strategies should be developed in modules to match the organisational units of the customer and to utilise limited objectives as a means of achieving success and raising organisational aspirations. They should focus on tangible problems and present solutions with which the customer organisation has some familiarity. Objectives should be approached singularly rather than as a multi-directional thrust. Even major programmes involving major system changes for greatest organisational acceptance should move through a progression of small increments.

Service strategies should have a dynamic structure of implementation, moving in successive stages through individual units of the customer's organisation. The nature of organisations is that of a coalition of individual members, each with individual as well as organisational goals, and who can be persuaded to respond only over an extended period of time. Strategy must establish their previous experience as initial reference points. It must also adapt to the anticipated future need. All this requires understanding the decision-making processes which take place within the customer's organisation.

To demonstrate, suppose that a supplying organisation is developing a strategy to establish more interdependent relationships with its major accounts in order to reduce costs. Within this objective, the role of customer service is to provide sufficient support to encourage customers to operate with extremely limited inventory in return for precisely controlled and delivered service support. Ultimately, the supplier will become the major source of supply for this product class. The elements of this strategy are to provide safety stock for the customer, tightly coordinated delivery and an efficient order-placement discipline within the customer's organisation. The customer's operating units are the inventory control and the receiving sections, merchandise buyers and the sales department.

To impose this strategy at one time might induce resistance within the customer's organisation because it constitutes too abrupt a change for the management of these sections. A series of steps must then be individually planned for each department.

For the inventory control manager, a series of stages could be programmed to reduce incrementally safety stocks on specific classes of items, beginning with low-turnover items, gradually turning towards high-turnover items, to the point that the customer carries no safety stock on his premises.

Instead of ordering individual line items, he might be persuaded to order in standardised quantities, then in item groups, ultimately in standardised modules. Receiving would be introduced to a precise delivery schedule and encouragement to process and place stocks in operating locations on prearranged schedules, then to receive these standard modules and to move these to locations without delay. Merchandise buyers could be introduced to buying codes as a first step, then to changes in ordering procedure and finally to changes in data acquisition and processing equipment. The sales force might be encouraged to specify minimum floor stocks, then to handle only modular orders, with special replacement ordering as the floor items are sold. Ultimately slow-turnover items could be sold from samples only, supported by special order procedures. At each stage, each department will be faced with a problem of adaptation of limited scope while it is adapting to progressively more radical changes in its operating environment. To manage all these changes simultaneously, to move a customer from one position towards another, requires intricate coordination.

All this planning is necessary because organisations are dealing with organisations. The rules of structured group behaviour do not encourage major jumps such as those anticipated with major innovative changes. On the other hand, permanent changes are for the most part incremental in nature. A succession of small, carefully-planned incremental changes can, however, lead to substantial progress over time.

Conclusion

Customer service is a system involving both the supplier and his customer in relationships surrounding the movement of products between them. Service in a strategic setting is one component in a larger set of comprehensive marketing relationships which are not always clearly perceived by either the originator or the recipient. Strategic objectives are concerned with customer response to specific aspects of service. These, in turn, are the output of organisations which respond in particular ways, depending on the environments in which they operate. Strategies involve the development of sets of options into meaningful alternatives; in the perspectives of service, these involve elements both internal to the organisations involved and their external links too. The service system links two organisations. To be successfully adopted and implemented, strategies must take account of the characteristics of organisational behaviour.

A customer service strategy in the full meaning of the phrase is almost conjectural. The normal strategic practice is to seek short-term solutions of limited scope — and measured by only the most tangible indicators of successful performance. The short-term is not enough. The short-term relationship implies a longer-term future, but this future is of necessity poorly defined. The market, technological and organisational environments are constantly changing. The essential strategic task is, therefore, to accept as a continuous process the examination and redefinition of the essential characteristics of this long-term relationship.

References

1. Christopher, M.G., J.L. Gattorna, D.L. Ray and D.W. Walters; *Cage Palletization in the U.K. Grocery Industry: An Evaluation of Total System Costs and Benefits* Report of a Study Commissioned by the Institute of Grocery Distribution and Undertaken by Cranfield School of Manangement, (January 1977).
2. Cyert, Richard M. and James G. March, *A Behavioral Theory of the Firm* (Englewood Cliffs, N.J.: Prentice Hall, Inc. 1963) pp.114-127 as cited in Frederick E. Webster and Yoram Wind, *Organizational Behavior* (Englewood Cliffs, N.J.: Prentice Hall, Inc. 1972), pp.68-70.
3. Day, George, 'Diagnosing the Product Portfolio', *Journal of Marketing*. (April 1977), pp.29-38.
4. Mickwitz, Gosta, *Marketing and Competition* (Helsingfors, Finland: Centraltruckeriet, 1959) as cited in Philip Kotler, *Marketing Decision Making* (New York: Holt, Rinehart and Winston, 1971), pp.62-63.
5. Hutchinson, W.H., and J.F. Stolle, 'How to Manage Customer Service, *Harvard Business Review*, Nov/Dec 1968.

8 Management control over customer service

Control over customer service can only be partial at best. If service is an adaptation of one system, the supplier's, to fit another, then the customer's part of the combined system is only subject to indirect influence. There is a further problem, however; the focus of the greater part of the discussion of customer service has taken the limited perspective of the immediate interface between systems, usually defined in terms of a limited set of parameters, such as product availability, delivery time and its variability. Strategy implies more than this, as we have seen in the previous chapter. A broad view of customer service, however, makes the service process much more difficult to control.

In this chapter, we wish to consider four specific topics. The discussion begins with the problem of control within a strategic context. It then proceeds to the approaches to control which are currently being used, including findings from study of the practices of six manufacturing firms. This discussion will then focus on development of control over customer service as strategy. Finally we will focus on the organisational issues involved.

Control problems in customer service

From a strategic perspective, customer service proceeds through a series of stages as shown in Figure 8.1. These are presented as a sequential process. In practice there would also be several feedback mechanisms between the stages involving the customer and the strategy and service parameters of the supplier.

The first stage begins with defining the objectives, which can usually be specified in terms of market share, profits or sales. Other objectives can usually be translated into these terms. These objectives then become the ultimate criteria against which service strategies should be evaluated. High levels of product availability by themselves may be laudable targets, but they may be dysfunctional criteria for a strategy except as means to an end. These objectives can be translated into more operational terms by considering the role of customer service within a larger marketing strategy. The purpose of service can be: (a) to change the customer's behaviour in some way in order to increase sales volume; (b) to reduce the costs of serving him; or (c) to retain his business by making it more attractive to him in terms of his internal costs.

These objectives can be translated into a variety of initiatives. These are typified hypothetically, for example by strategies such as reducing customer inventories by carrying their safety stock and offering fast delivery, or by developing standard ordering systems which reduce the customer's clerical costs. Strategies considered as entities can become broadly developed and thus difficult to control by direct statistical measures. These strategies must then be measured in operational terms such as statistical data on product availability, or costs per order incurred by the customer. These measures, however, are not functional elements of a service strategy, and cannot be considered as strategies in their own right. Unless they contribute to a coherent design, they may not produce a coordinated impact on the customer.

At the other end of the sequence, the customer is inexorably

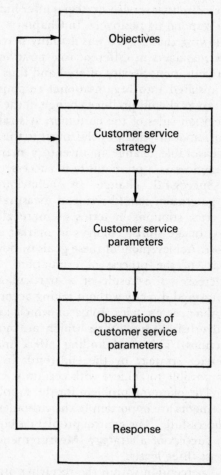

Figure 8.1 The response to deviations can either be a revision of the strategy or a reformulation of the service objectives or a combination of both

involved in the success of service strategies. He must first perceive that service strategies offer him favourable advantages in responding positively. In Chapter 4, evidence was presented showing that service was actually perceived in different terms by managers in different role positions within the customer's organisation. Service offered and thus perceived must then be translated into organisational response. A successful service strategy should produce change in the operating practices and decision rules of the customer. A strategy designed to reduce customer inventory by shifting it to the supplier should result in measurable change in inventory management and ordering practices as a prerequisite to success.

Successful change in behaviour of the customer's organisation should result in measurable response to the new service stimulus in terms of more global measures, such as patronage shifts, changes in market shares, or reductions in cost. Achievement of these goals is, however, the most difficult part of the process of evaluation. The question 'Do sales increase as a result of a particular strategy?', cannot be answered directly without taking account of all other potential influences on sales, some of which are controllable, such as advertising, and others which are not, such as competitors' actions. This confounding effect makes the evaluation of service strategy by the end-result in most situations almost impossible to achieve with certainty.

The planning problem for the supplier is to determine what elements are important to the customer and how to apply them successfully. The control problem is how to measure the degree of success of a strategy. Measurement must take place on at least three levels:

1   perception within the receiving organisation
2   the organisational response
3   the evaluation of the overall goals of the strategy.

The differences in perception within the organisation present the first level of difficulty. One objective of marketing a service programme must be to achieve consensus, within the customer's organisation, for without it there cannot be successful evaluation of service strategy.

Determining organisational response also presents considerable difficulty. One problem is the time-lag involved. There is organisational inertia in making changes, not only in decision rules for operations but in changing the orientation of managers. A service strategy to reduce inventory may create uneasiness with inventory control managers. They must build experience with new systems before they can reduce the discomfort caused by attempting to operate with less stock on hand. At the same time, evidence of change may reflect factors other than service policies per se. Inventories may be reduced as response to suppliers' service offerings, but they might also be reduced by policies stemming from high interest rates.

The concept of market response invites a further difficulty in measurement. Response implies a monotone functional relationship between service levels and sales. Although the actual form of the response function can only be established through formal experimentation, no one wishes to experiment with a customer. The concept, however, is difficult to discard. Managerial behaviour implies that this abstract relationship enters into the service decision calculus even though the concept of response may never be explicitly identified.

The evaluation of service strategy through achievement of overall strategic goals, such as sales, market share or profits, becomes even more difficult. It is small wonder that firms faced with this problem will avoid the problems of measurement at a strategic level, to focus on the more limited area of operational measurement. Here the results can be made with more clarity and less ambiguity, although they may reflect in the end a short-sightedness as well.

Further evidence from the study

All six companies in the study used formal standards of customer service. These were normally expressed in terms of average lead time, product availability and similar measures. Only one company, however, displayed evidence of a customer service strategy in which service elements were combined into an integrated offering to the market. This company used a set of standards as a guaranteed measure of performance to be used in negotiation with individual customers. This contract approach offers several strategic advantages for both the supplier and its customers. The sales force was instructed to incorporate service performance into its presentations. The standards also became internal controls for warehouse and delivery operations. Third, these standards functioned to communicate a level of expectation about service to the customer, establishing a basis on which negotiation could take place for higher levels. The contractual terms also provided communication to the customer for his own inventory planning and receiving operations.

In general, the remaining firms appeared to lack comprehensive service reporting systems which would be capable of providing management with the information necessary to manage service effectively. However, the initiative to develop these systems had been taken in advance of a formal concept of customer service management. Several reporting programmes were just starting at the time of the study. Below are listed the titles of the reports encountered:

1   order cycle time analysis
2   order cycle time components analysis
3   percentage of orders delivered within promised delivery dates
4   product availability analysis — percentage of items ordered delivered from stock
5   balance order analysis
6   order accuracy analysis
7   order deletions and returns analysis
8   order status analysis.

At the time of the study, the reporting systems however, were either erratic in their performance or were too new to permit an overall control over customer service performance. For example, all six companies had measured order cycle time performance. However, as a general statement, the degree of commitment to these measures as indicated by the frequency of measurement of actual performance indicated that this control was not extensively used.

None of the six companies had established a position for customer service management with either responsibility or authority for the activities that determine customer service performance. Because of the interfunctional involvement in service performance across the company, this is more than a task for the distribution manager alone. This responsibility typically was diffused throughout the organisation without formal coordination or control. Related to this is the lack of a single point of contact for customers concerning their orders. In one company, the customer had to make three separate contacts on occasion in order to interrogate the company about his order status.

Operational measures

Customer service has developed in industry not in a strategic context but in a much more limited setting. It has been reactive rather than innovative. Service which exceeds the norm for the specific market in which the firm was engaged was considered to be wasteful. It has also been oriented towards the *production* of distribution, rather than the *marketing* of distribution as a service product. The result has been that distribution management has tended to think of service in terms of a limited set of dimensions dealing with product availability and delivery time, which can be measured with relative ease. Because these are at the core of the interface relationships of most distribution systems, they provide a logical place to provide a discussion of service control.

There are three fundamental questions which must be answered in developing an adequate control system for customer service:

What dimensions are important and therefore what information should be provided?

Who should receive this information?

How should it be presented?

A distinction can be made here between primary and

secondary data. Primary data are collected for a specific purpose. Secondary data are collected for one purpose and are then adapted to another application. Most of the data necessary for operational control are already captured within the order-processing system as a result of the normal operations of the system. The remainder of the secondary data may require some cooperation by wholesalers and delivering carriers. Even though this latter data can also often be considered as primary data, here, too, it is often collected by these other agencies for their own purposes.

Product availability

Product availability is the dominant dimension of customer service in many companies. The definition of availability can, however, be interpreted in a variety of ways: (a) the proportion of items which can be filled from inventory; (b) the proportion of orders which can be filled completely from inventory; (c) the proportion of customer orders shipped completely within a specified number of days after receipt of the order in the warehouse; (d) the proportion of order lines processed which can be filled completely.

The list can be quite extensive. For example, Brown (1, Chapter 10) lists a series of six decision rules which can be used to determine service:

1 specify the service level for all items of inventory
2 minimise back-orders for a given investment
3 specify safety stocks by a safety factor
4 specify safety stock by weeks of supply
5 minimise the number of shortage occurrences
6 minimise the number of transactions short.

Items (3) and (4) appear to be merely translations of other statistical measures. The others, however, reflect assumptions about customer behaviour which should be part of a larger set of strategies. The data to monitor stock availability is potentially capturable during the order process. To this extent then, inventory is the most convenient starting point for the development of service control.

Order cycle time

This is another important operational service variable. The total order cycle time can be defined as the total time elapsed between the placing of an order by a customer and the delivery of the order to the customer's premises. The order cycle can be divided into its time-components, some of which are supplier-determined, others customer-determined. Four components are normally identified: (a) order acquisition and transmission — customer determined; (b) order processing — supplier determined; (c) order picking and shipping — supplier determined; (d) delivery — supplier determined.
In addition, there may be a time lapse between receipt and updating of customer records.

Orders may be generated either by the customer's organisation or by the salesman. Customer delays are normally not controllable or monitored. Transmission time, however, can be changed by choosing the mode of transmission; control of the elapsed time is then beyond the domain of either party. Data on transmission time can be captured on the order document, provided that elapsed times are entered.

Order-processing time is the supplier's responsibility and should be available within the computer files. Similarly, the warehouse activities can be monitored through documentation of order receipt, picking and shipping dates. The actual delivery is more difficult to measure, particularly if for-hire carriers are used, because information becomes more difficult to collect. Two methods are commonly used: (a) return postcard forms indicating date of receipt; (b) dated signatures on carrier delivery documents.

The data thus collected can be used for statistical analysis to identify average processing times for individual components and the sources of variability. This then permits focusing on more narrowly-defined problems, such as the policies of batch-processing of orders, stocking-out, or holding orders in order to ensure complete delivery as deliberate decisions to hold orders to stabilise warehouse workloads, and ensure high utilisation of the delivery vehicle.

Other types of information

In some industries, another relevant measure of service performance is the proportion of items deleted (because of stock-outs) or returned because of picking errors. There may be a variety of reasons for these to occur, some of which may not be under the control of the supplier. Analysis to identify these reasons is therefore useful. Table 8.1 shows an example of this analysis for one of the companies in the survey. This particular company operates a large number of local depots which are in turn supplied from a smaller network of factories. The analysis permits management to identify problem areas in what would otherwise be a difficult system to analyse.

Problems of strategic control over customer service

Operational measures of customer service can be invoked without formal statements about strategic objectives or grand designs in the market place. This is not to say that strategy is not present. Even purely reactive intentions imply strategies of competitive parity and maintenance of market share. The alternative to implied strategies is to set forth deliberate strategies, to be exercised through carefully designed combinations of service elements to influence the behaviour of customers. Strategies in this area are not easy to implement, partly because they are difficult to control. In this section the strategy problem will be outlined, followed by development of a framework for approaching the control problems of strategy.

The concept of customer service strategy as such has received little attention. In many respects, service suggests another variation on market strategies. The principal change is the dual product characteristic: service product offered in conjunction with the tangible product that the customer desires. The development of control for these strategies should therefore also borrow heavily from marketing. The form of the analysis should be regarded as a tentative approach, which will be developed further as a more formal approach to service strategy itself develops.

Table 8.1 Cumulative analysis of short deliveries, cancellations and redeliveries by reason — National total of all depots period 7, 197-

		Product Group		
		A	B	C
1 Short deliveries and cancellations				
A) By distribution action				
Damaged goods	Orders	331	46	26
	Units	552	69	35
Faulty stock ordering	Orders	40	4	7
	Units	90	24	35
Other distribution errors	Orders	5931	976	784
	Units	11433	2873	2386
Percentage	Orders	6.08	5.07	5.14
Percentage	Units	0.36	0.50	0.34
B) By sales action				
Incorrect delivery instructions	Orders	58	11	9
	Units	254	74	19
Part order refused by customer	Orders	499	65	48
	Units	4776	809	430
Order cancelled by customer	Orders	820	244	133
	Units	28206	6160	6108
Sale of withdrawn lines	Orders	2153	177	126
	Units	4938	947	550
Percentage	Orders	3.41	2.45	1.98
Percentage	Units	1.13	1.35	1.00
C) By production and others				
Stock not available	Orders	7920	1218	970
	Units	19466	5646	4292
Unavoidable stock delays	Orders	644	145	210
	Units	1718	686	739
Percentage	Orders	8.29	6.77	7.43
Percentage	Units	0.63	1.07	0.71
2 Complete orders returned for redelivery due to:				
A) Distribution	Orders	667	174	135
	Units	16480	3473	4165
B) Sales	Orders	2281	574	275
	Units	68857	13650	5020
C) Others	Orders	93	37	26
	Units	3177	2655	1503
Percentage	Orders	2.93	3.88	2.74
Percentage	Units	2.64	3.35	1.51
Total orders delivered		99627	19177	15311
Total units delivered		3190472	551964	680665
Total orders taken		103488	20206	15880
Total units ordered		3350445	589035	705947

The strategy problem

As Figure 8.1 has described the control problem, service starts with strategic objectives and the results of strategy can only be evaluated in terms of those objectives. The problem with matching performance with objectives is that no matter how specific the objective may be, i.e. the intended effect, the cause cannot be established with certainty. There are many variables interacting on market performance objectives such as share, sales or profits. Other decisions within the company, such as changes in pricing or advertising, decisions by the buyer to change his stock reorder policies, the impact of competitors, and changes in the macrodistribution environment in the form of changes in the economy and the transportation structure for example, all influence the outcome in terms of measurable results. The result is a confounding effect that in the end says very little about the success or failure of service strategies *per se*.

If service strategies cannot be measured by the final result, then we are forced to turn to measuring intervening variables and the performance of strategy on these variables. The dilemma is that, apart from simple operational performance variables discussed in the previous section, there is no universally acceptable structure which can be applied.

How can we select intervening variables as a proxy measure of the success of failure of a strategy? The direct analogy from marketing is presented in an article by Crawford [3] who was attempting to define success or failure at an early stage in new-product introduction. He developed his own analogy in the launch of a missile, identifying the dimensions of new-product adoption as counterparts to the missile's trajectory. These would be logical indicators of early success or, conversely, of the early need for corrective action. In short, development and control of service strategy requires signals which will clearly indicate the success or suggested direction for remedial action.

Potential framework

The first premise is that customer service is 'a product; a change in the level or dimensions of service is analogous to a new product which must be launched successfully in the market place and be accepted by customers if it is to be effective. The number of customers, at least in intermediate markets, is sufficiently small to monitor limited, individual adoption processes more closely than consumer-goods suppliers can do with final consumers in a mass market. The second premise is that organisations, like individual consumers, will follow a series of logical steps referred to in the adoption of products in the marketing literature as 'the hierarchy of effects'. Although there are several variations on the same theme, the fundamental process begins with awareness of the product, moves the consumer through heightening interest into a motivational stage, producing behaviour of trial and adoption [6]. Some versions of this model will also include a post-use evaluation process. There is no direct research available to cite a transference to inter-organisational exchanges such as those involving customer service. However, it suggests a plausible framework for the introduction of intervening variables. Adaptation of the hierarchy of effects process to an organisational service context is shown in Table 8.2.

Table 8.2 A framework for customer service control

'Hierarchy of effects' stages	Service response stages
Awareness	Organisational perception
Interest	Recognition of pay-offs
Evaluation	Organisational evaluation
Decision	Changes in operating practices
Evaluation	Organisational recognition of advantages of new policy

The first stage is to ensure that service changes are perceived within the customer's organisation. As we saw in Chapter 4, these perceptions will vary by role position within the organisation. The first stage in a customer service strategy is to create awareness of the change, both as a proposed standard and as performance. This may involve assisting the internal communication network of the customer as discussed in Chapter 6, and possibly even providing the standards of measurement. The second stage establishes that all participants are aware of the potential advantages in accepting the new service strategy. This suggests a promotional campaign through direct contact to individuals within the organisation, and which would be measured through achievement of acceptable attitudes toward the programme.

The third stage is evaluation by the customer, where advantages and disadvantages can be compared. Because this is a definite progression towards a point of decision, this may be the most difficult step to achieve and may require substantive active selling assistance at a technical level.

The fourth stage, the actual decision, is manifested in changes in decision rules and other operating practices of the customer's organisation which reflect adopting a new service.

The final stage is to ensure favourable post-experience evaluation. Service is part of an on-going system. Service must be performed with consistency (which involves internal controls by the supplier) and with visible measures of performance which can be used by the customer. These measures can become the basis of maintaining the service product on an on-going basis. The process should be reinforced through frequent reporting by the supplier about his actual performance.

The hierarchy of effects provides not a set of strategies by itself but a set of measurement points. Management must decide on the level of awareness and the direction and level of diffusion of information to the customer. Coupled with this is the necessity to study the needs of the customer so that both the elements of strategy and the criteria for evaluation represent useful dimensions of service. These steps are similar in concept to a conventional sales campaign, with the aim of establishing changes in the service relationship which advance the needs of the customer as well as those of the supplier.

The process then moves to the customer's organisation. The evidence of the nature of the decision may be communicated directly, or indirectly through actions taken in response. Observation of changes in communication, differences in order patterns and other similar indicators would indicate acceptance. Service is designed, however, to hold customers over extended periods of time. Success must be measured over the long-term, although the actual measurement itself becomes more difficult.

Organisational issues

The ambiguous nature of the customer service relationship creates difficulties within the supplier's organisation, both at operating level first, followed by organisational issues in control over strategy.

Operating responsibility for customer service

Who should take the necessary action to ensure performance in customer service? This is one of the major difficulties in implementing customer service policies. At the present time, there appears to be little consensus. Much depends on the organisational orientation towards service. One recent survey indicated that service as a function reports to physical distribution, logistics or material management departments 42 per cent of the time for reporting firms in the U.S., and to sales or marketing 23 per cent of the time [4]. The remainder used other reporting relationships. Presumably location within a sales or marketing department suggests a more outward orientation, but this is conjectural. There was also little unanimity among the surveyed companies about which functions should be included as part of the customer service area. The central function of most customer service organisations appears to be order entry and processing, combined with a number of related activities such as order status reporting, handling complaints and expediting back orders.

The interfunctional nature of customer service creates an organisational dilemma. The nature of customer service as an integrative activity implies that the only effective hierarchical control comes at the level of the chief executive officer of the organisation. At a lower level in the organisation, the problem is one of coordination rather than authority.

The first step in analysing the structure of the customer service organisation is to identify the basic activities involved and then to define them in relation to other functions within the company. For example, warehouse operations, delivery services and quality control all have an impact on customer service, but are normally under the jurisdiction of other departments. The customer service unit, however, should have the authority to initiate or propose corrective actions which cut across functional lines The role of the customer service manager is simultaneously to integrate or coordinate while performing as a line manager with direct authority over his own operations. If the customer service function is to operate with effectiveness, it requires the recognition and support of high level sponsorship within the organisation, otherwise the service system tends to dissolve into components operating with relative autonomy.

As far as relationships exist with marketing or sales, there appears to be an almost complete barrier between sales on the one hand and distribution on the other. Sales tends to avoid becoming involved with distribution problems; distribution tends to be oriented towards its own operations as a production effort and seldom seeks out customers. The differences in orientation tend to suppress communication between these areas.

The customer, however, may not take the same view. More likely, he will consider sales and distribution as parts of a common system. Managers on the supply side may be reluctant to integrate in order to serve the customer, but this may not match the expectations of the market which fails to recognise these internal differences.

Strategic control for customer service

Customer service management and strategy are new concepts in organisations. The roles are not firmly defined, but are in evolution. In some respects, customer service has been identified with the acceptance of the logistics concept inside the organisation. Howver, as we have suggested, it has broader ramifications.

The strategic tasks of a customer service manager are to plan, i.e. to develop alternatives and the means to fulfil them, to monitor their performance and to audit them to establish the current service position of the company. Planning and monitoring have already been discussed. The concept of the customer service audit is new, however, and deserves some expansion. Again, we will borrow from general marketing concepts to suggest the nature and content of the audit process.

The concept of an audit in both marketing and physical distribution is an answer to the question which Christopher *et al.* [2, p.47] have posited as 'where are we now?' Kotler in the marketing context defines it as:

> A marketing audit is a periodic, comprehensive, systematic and independent examination of the organisation's marketing environment, internal marketing system and specific marketing activities with a view to determining problem areas and recommending a corrective action plan to improve the organisation's overall marketing effectiveness. [5, p.448].

If we substitute the words 'customer service' for 'marketing', we have a concept of what is involved in a customer service audit. The important aspect of this definition is that it stresses four major components: the environment, the internal system, activities and recommendations. In a period when the concept of customer service is in rapid evolution towards goals only dimly seen, the audit may prove to be the most useful tool in management of the service process.

The environment issues surround the service relationship. The changing characteristics of markets, shifts in market structure, and the characteristics of customers, all point to the need for extensive and frequent reconsideration of service. The state of competition can always be assumed to become more intense than it is today. Other elements will form the basis on which an evaluation of service must rest. These include changes in the political environment and regulation of business, the development or discontinuance of transportation options, other technology such as computer and material handling systems, the state of the economy, and the changing nature of channel relationships.

Four aspects of the internal system itself should be examined critically: the objectives, the organisation commitment to a planned programme, implementation and the location of organisational responsibility. Even to define the system itself becomes a useful task, as our experience with the six companies has shown.

A detailed review should survey the operational measures available and being used to monitor service performance, such as indicators of product availability and order cycle time, and other measures more specific to the situation. It should also examine the specific procedures used to fill orders. To trace the order fulfilment system may identify points of delay which might otherwise go unobserved.

Service should also be examined from the perspective of the customer. One obvious way is to survey customers directly to identify direct indications of satisfaction or its lack. Other measures, such as retail market audit data, may also indicate indirectly where service difficulties lie through store coverage and inventory data. Finally, measures of market performance such as market share may identify areas for further questioning. Data such as these indicators may not identify the problem but they could indicate the correct place for further questions.

A service audit should not end with the present system and currently available options. Advantages for one service system at one point in time may not be relevant at another.

Finally, an audit should also examine the costs of service. As these change, other approaches to service may become desirable.

An audit thus provides a thorough examination of the entire context within which service operates. It is, however, an investigation at one point in time. The findings should not be considered as a permanent landmark, but as progressive indicators of change tracked through successive audits.

Who should take charge of the auditing process and strategic planning for customer service? Once again there has been no clearly defined answer from industry practice. Because it involves customer relationships, it falls within the area of marketing. However, it also involves distribution activities directly, and possibly production activities as well. In performing customer service audits for the six companies in the study, the individuals assigned to coordinate our activities with the firm were predominantly, but not exclusively, from marketing areas. In two cases, they came from distribution. Never were they from production, which indicates where the sponsorship of service lies.

In a modern organisation, it does not appear to be possible to point to any hierarchical position which would become specifically involved in the full extent of service strategy. This then places a burden on the strategist/manager to coordinate and persuade rather than to order service policies into effect.

Conclusion

The topic of control in an area as open to further development as customer service is almost premature. We have seen that the development of rigorous controls can only be applied to the internal operations of the supplier. If there is a customer service strategy, how can its success or failure be measured without the presence of indicators? Strategy therefore requires the development of structured market-oriented approaches to provide benchmarks. Finally, the development of strategy implies a centre from which strategy can emanate. This may prove to be the crucial element in the creation, management and control of the process as a strategic element in the enterprise.

References

1. Brown, Robert C. *Modern Materials Management,* New York, John Wiley, 1977.
2. Christopher, Martin, David Walters and John Gattorna, *Distribution: Planning and Control* (Farnborough, England: Gower Press, 1977).
3. Crawford, Merle, 'Trajectory Theory of Goal Setting and New Products', *Journal of Market Research,* (May 166), pp.117-121.
4. Davis, Herbert W., 'Customer Service — an Update on Organisation Standards and Performance Evaluation, *Proceedings of the 1971 Annual Meeting,* National Council of Physical Distribution Management (Chicago, Ill.: NCPDM, 1975.), pp.139-168.
5. Kotler, Philip, *Marketing Management, Analysis, Planning and Control,* (Englewood Cliffs, N.J., Prentice-Hall, 1976).
6. Lavidge, Robert J. and Gary A. Steiner, 'A Model for the Predictive Measurement of Advertising "Effectiveness", *Journal of Marketing,* (October 1961), pp.59-62.

9   How to evaluate customer service*

One of the pervading issues throughout this book has been the question of the assessment of the impact of customer service upon the market. As we have seen there are many facets to distribution service and the reactions of the customer to the service he receives is itself based upon a blend of objective and subjective evaluations. It thus becomes a task of some complexity to measure and interpret the market response to customer service.

We have laid great emphasis in this book on the crucial importance of service in marketing and distribution strategy. However, many companies have no clearly-defined policy towards customer service; indeed, in many cases, customer service is only narrowly perceived in a technical or after-sales sense. The wider view of customer service, advocated here and adopted by a handful of innovative companies, brings together all the points of contact with the customer in terms of delivery frequency and lead-time, back-up inventory, responsiveness to complaints, technical service and a host of other aspects. Obviously creating an integrated and cohesive service involving all these elements is a task requiring careful analysis and planning. Likewise as customer service is clearly a major cost element in any company's marketing effort, it requires a constant evaluation in terms of how well it is meeting the desired objectives set for it and how the actual costs of the

* This chapter draws on material presented in Christopher, M.G., Walters, D.W. and Gattorna, J., *Distribution Planning & Control*, Gower Press 1977, and in Elliott, C.K. and Christopher, M.G., *Research Methods in Marketing*, Holt, Rinehart & Winston 1973.

programme compare with the planned costs. The monitoring and control function is therefore one of comparison between actual and desired objectives, with the aim of identifying and remedying the causes of any divergence between the two.

Control mechanisms for customer service can be simple or complex, they can either be based upon a regular review with management intervention when key indications suggest that deviations between actual outputs and planned targets are occurring, or they can be based upon self-regulating mechanisms that operate according to prescribed decision rules. An example of this latter would be a computerised inventory control and reordering system.

From the discussion so far it is evident that there are two key elements in the control system. One is the 'monitor' and the other is the 'standard'.

The service monitor

Setting up the service monitor should be a systematic procedure. Heskett *et al* [2] suggest a sequence which, slightly modified, would be:
1 identify all important logistics cost categories along with other inputs of effort which the organisation incurs
2 institute systems and procedures for the collection of this cost data
3 identify and collect output data
4 prepare a set of desired measures by which the logistics activities within the organisation might be evaluated
5 set up a mechanism for the regular presentation of status reports.

This procedure begins with the recognition that customer service costs, wherever they occur, should be flushed out and brought together. Typically, traditional accounting systems will not be capable of providing the data in the form in which it is required. Many customer service costs will be lost in the 'general overheads' of the business, e.g. order-processing costs.

Designing the procedures for the collection of this data is therefore no easy task.

Identifying and collecting output data may also be problematic. Output data in the customer service context are concerned with revenue, thus the problem becomes one of pinpointing the extent to which the service package has resulted in the generation of revenue. Obviously this is not possible and so, assuming a relationship between revenue generation and service level, managers often use the latter as a surrogate measure. Hence measures such as order cycle time, percentage of back-orders, consistency of delivery lead-times and so on have to be used. Fairly simple recording and reporting systems will normally be sufficient to generate the required data. For example, regular samples can be taken of individual customer orders to check on order cycle lead-time, likewise for the percentage of orders met from stock and so on.

Measuring performance within the logistics organisation involves the collection, on the same regular basis, of such data as warehouse costs (handling, storage) and utilisation, transportation costs and utilisation, inventory costs and order-processing costs. This data is often conveniently presented in the form of ratios, e.g. cost per case, cost per ton-mile, etc.

In all this data collection activity the key requirement is to ensure that they are collected according to compatible bases. Often data exist relating to these various activity centres but on a non-comparable basis: in some cases information may be available on a quarterly basis relating to sales areas, other information is on a weekly basis relating to customer accounts, still other data relates to factory shipments to customer accounts, still other data relates to factory shipments on a product basis. Bringing all this data together and reconciling it to a common base is generally not possible. In most cases devising an effective logistics service control system requires the redesign of data-gathering procedures, which can present a major stumbling block. Management objections to such a redesign can be overcome if the pay-offs of having an effective control system can be emphasised.

The reporting format of such a monitoring system will vary

according to the requirements of the individual company. In terms of the preparation of such reports it is important that the interval between reports should be short enough to enable changes in inputs and system parameters to be made promptly. Taking action on information received too late can sometimes lead to a worsening of the situation.

The peculiar dynamics of systems are such that 'leads and lags' in stimulus and response will mean that fine-tuning of the system is rarely possible. While it may not be possible, or indeed necessary, to have 'real-time' reporting systems, it is necessary to recognise that information has a value which is inversely related to time — the more out-of-date it is, the less value it has. One can in fact identify within a given situation the frequency with which information relating to logistics service is required. For example, data on stock-outs, back-orders, warehouse replenishments and so on may be appropriate on a daily basis; inventory levels and order intake could be collected on a weekly basis; order-cycle lead-times and consistency on a monthly basis and so on.

Setting service standards

In order that control can be exercised it is obviously necessary that the data resulting from the monitor be compared to some standard of desired performance. This is the case for both the outputs of the system and also for the internal activities of the process itself. Many firms have established cost standards for the basic distribution activities such as transportation and warehousing. Fewer companies, however, set standards for service outputs.

The derivation of service standards must obviously be related to the objectives or missions of the logistics system that should previously have been identified. In some cases missions may be stated in terms of the provision of specific levels of service, in other cases service may be implied but not strictly defined. The service standard is simply the operational means whereby the level is measured.

Examples of such standards could be:

Service element	Service standard
Order cycle lead-time	Nine days from receipt of order to customer taking delivery of complete consignment

Order transmission:	2 days
Order processing:	3 days
Delivery:	4 days

Service element	Service standard
Consistency of lead-time	At least 95 per cent of all deliveries will be made between seven days and eleven days. The remaining 5 per cent to be made between six and twelve days.
Inventory levels	Using an ABC classification system inventory levels will be set to achieve: A items: 95 per cent of all orders to be met from stock. B items: 85 per cent of all orders to be met from stock. C items: 80 per cent of all items to be met from stock.
Accuracy in order-filling	Orders to be filled with 99.5 per cent accuracy
Damage in transit	Damage in transit not to exceed 0.5 per cent of order value

In addition standards could be set for specific customer accounts or groups, individual products and so on.

These service standards would complement the cost standards which have been derived by the traditional costing procedures. Cost standards by themselves are of little value as they relate only to the way in which inputs are utilised rather than the way in which outputs are generated. The two taken together, however, enable a cost/benefit approach to customer service to be made operational by providing an understanding of how the customer service outputs are related to the various logistics inputs.

The control of customer service is made complete by the comparison of the data revealed by the monitor with the prescribed cost and service standards. Any variation between actual and standard will need to be accounted for and if necessary acted upon.

Surveying customer opinion

The measures of performance just described are essentially *internal* and an audit of customer service would be incomplete without a clear indication of how the customers themselves react to that service.

Much of this book has been devoted to reporting the conclusions drawn from an empirical examination of a number of companies' policies towards customer service and the reaction of the recipients to it. In the earlier chapters, data was presented which was gleaned from respondents by survey methods. The methods used varied considerably but they all took as their starting point the view that *direct* questioning was inappropriate. There is no point in asking the question 'Is the service you receive from the XYZ company satisfactory?' or, even worse, 'How would you react to a reduction in the level of service?'. Most people when asked questions like that tend to emphasise the need for improvements and to consider current service offerings as adequate rather than satisfactory. In reality, of course, it can often be the case that the service they receive is taken for granted and that reductions in that service, up to a point, might not even be noticed.

Alternative approaches, relying upon indirect questioning or experimentation, must therefore be used in any attempt to explore the true response to customer service.

Indirect approaches

In any survey of customer opinion one of the first requirements is to avoid conditioning the responses of the respondent by the questions themselves. Thus it is of little value to ask a customer to compare different suppliers according to the lead-time they offer, if lead-time is not a dimension used by that respondent in his personal evaluation of suppliers. Whilst the customer may happily answer the question, the answer will not necessarily signify anything. It is important therefore as a first step to ascertain the key dimensions used by the customers themselves in *their* evaluation of customer service rather than what we, the survey designers, consider the key dimensions to be.

The ideal approach to designing customer survey tools is to begin by collecting from a limited sample of customers their own 'vocabulary' of evaluative constructs concerning customer service. In other words, what are the issues that they see as important in the context of customer service, in their own language? One technique which the authors have used with some success is the method known as the 'Repertory Grid'.

The technique is fairly straightforward to administer. There are a number of variants, but the usual procedure is to prepare a set of cards on which are written or depicted the stimuli for investigation. thus, in this case, the researcher might present the sample of customers individually with a set of cards on each of which is written the name of a competing supplier and on one our own name. Three cards are then selected at random from the pack and the respondent is asked to state, in the context of their service offering, which two of the three are more similar — and why. He might, for example, answer that the two similar ones tend to be more reliable on delivery than the third. Thus the first construct to be elicited is 'delivery reliability'.

The next step is to ask the respondent to take the remaining pack of cards and to categorise them according to this identified dimension, i.e. good delivery reliability — poor delivery reliability. Following this, another random triad of cards is presented to the respondent and another dimension elicited, on the basis of which the remaining cards are sorted.

This procedure is followed until further triads produce no additional constructs. By repeating the procedure with further respondents from the sample it is possible to identify those dimensions which occur most frequently. These dimensions can then become the foundation for the questionnaire design, in the knowledge that they have meaning to the respondents, that they are relevant and, in particular, that they are couched in language that the respondents themselves use.

A further indirect approach to identifying customers' reactions to different service offerings is 'conjoint scaling' or 'trade-off analysis' [3]. This was the technique used in the studies described in Chapter 4 of this book. The basic idea underlying this technique is that whilst it is difficult, if not impossible, to get customers to evaluate various attributes of service on quantified scales they are quite capable of saying 'this combination of attributes is better than that'. For example if asked to choose between 24-hour service on 90 per cent of the items they order as against 48-hour service on 99 per cent, they can usually do so. By using conjoint scaling methods the analyst is able to quantify the 'weight' or the value that the respondent is placing on each attribute. Thus, in this case, to what extent the respondent is 'trading off' stock availability against delivery time can be precisely assessed.

Experimentation

In a sense, the only way to see how a customer will react to a service offering or a change in that offering is to go out into the market place and observe their behaviour. This of course can be problematical. We might suspect, for example, that our current level of service is too high. If we then decide to reduce it and to observe the market reaction we may find that it works against us and that we are losing real sales.

To avoid the risk of outcomes such as these it is necessary to perform *experiments*. Experimentation in marketing is not quite the precise test that we imagine it to be in scientific laboratory situations but it can provide us with valuable clues about customer reaction. Experimentation has the advantage of allowing the analyst to make changes in the variables being studied whilst controlling any other variables that might affect the outcome.

There are, however, a number of disadvantages associated with experimentation. Unfortunately, like so many problems involving cause and effect, it is rarely possible through simple observation to identify with certainty the underlying nature of causal processes. To say that A causes, or has some effect, on B requires a certitude that all other possible elements in the process have been identified and accounted for. The distribution manager attempting to assess the impact of a changed service level on the sales of his product needs to know more than just the 'before' and 'after' sales levels. Were any other marketing variables changed over the period of study? Was the competitive situation in any way different? And what would have happened to sales anyway if service had been left unchanged? Alternatively, if both service levels and price were simultaneously changed, how is the manager to separate the effects of these individual changes? Could there also have been interaction between these elements, thus producing a total effect that is greater or less than the individual effects? Clearly the problem assumes different proportions as these and other questions are asked.

To surmount these problems involves the distribution analyst assuming the stance of a scientist in the best tradition of empirical enquiry, using methodology directly akin to that employed in the laboratory. The difficulty is of course that whereas the scientist can utilise pure and exact inputs in a controlled environment and utilise sensitive and accurate measuring devices, the distribution analyst is working in a situation a good deal less perfect. Nevertheless the principles of laboratory experimentation are of considerable value to distribution research.

The experimental process is simple in concept. The experimenter examining a situation attempts to manipulate the inputs (independent variable or 'treatments') in order to observe the effect on the output (dependent variable). Observed variation in an output may take any of three forms:

1 *primary variation:* variation in the output resulting from changes in the identified inputs, e.g. sales increasing as a result of a service change.
2 *secondary variation:* variation in the output resulting from changes in unidentified or exogenous variables, e.g. sales increasing as a result of the weather, rather than the new service level.
3 *error variation:* variation in the output resulting from imperfect experimental conditions, e.g. measurement errors.

In the experiment itself the sources of variation are as far as possible separated in order that the primary variation may be identified. To achieve this it is necessary to introduce control into the experimental situation. The aim of this control is to enable the results of the experiment to be compared with an identical situation where no experiment was performed. Thus the manufacturer wishing to test a revised service might select two carefully matched shops, one selling the product with the existing service level and the other selling the product at the old level. In this way, secondary variations could be reduced or eliminated. Measurement error in the two situations would be constant and thus would be allowed for.

Figure 9.1 Paradigm of the experimental method

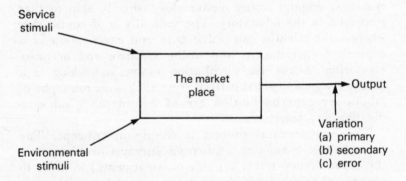

Figure 9.1 suggests a paradigm of the experimental method in such situations. It will be clear that whilst the experiment may show relationships between inputs and outputs in quantitative terms, e.g. a 1 per cent increase in A results in a 0.5 per cent increase in B, it will not say why this should be so. In the experiment the marketing situation is very much a 'black-box' of which the contents and their arrangement are unknown.

Such experiments are subject to complex distortions. There is the problem of lagged relationships; for example, if availability of a brand were to be improved for a month and a record kept on sales during the period, it is probably that the measured level of sales would considerably understate the true effect of the improved availability because of the likelihood of a delayed response. Other, less obvious, lags are widespread in marketing relationships and failure to recognise these lags could make the results of an experiment meaningless.

Another major problem in the design of such experiments is in the vital area of control when matched samples or special geographical locations are called for. For example, in the experiment to test the effect of service changes the manufacturer might decide to offer one service level in one area and a different one in another area. In order to minimise secondary variations the two locations would have to be carefully matched; the characteristics of the populations in terms of their shopping behaviour should be the same before the test, the areas should receive identical marketing support, such as advertising. In fact to achieve a perfect matching would probably be impossible, because of the plethora of secondary environmental stimuli.

Once the experiment is under way there may be unexpected localised changes in the experimental environment; in one of the two areas in the service experiment, for example, a competitor may start to run a money-off offer which will immediately distort the results of the experiment.

Operationally, too, there are problems associated with experimentation. Not many manufacturers, for example, would be prepared to reduce service in one area simply to test its effect! Perhaps the biggest drawback to marketing experimentation is the cost; it is very easy to run up huge bills with no firm promise of any commensurate pay-off. The small-scale laboratory simulation is not always possible, and if a negative effect is achieved in a marketing experiment real sales are being lost.

These drawbacks are mentioned as a caveat at this stage and must be constantly in mind as specific experimental designs are discussed.

The design of the experiment is of crucial importance. The very essence of experimentation is that the design will be of such a form that the results of the experiment will be valid. The experimental design involves the specification of procedures for manipulation of the independent variables and for the assignation of subjects. Some designs are termed 'quasi-experimental' because the investigator is not able to specify the manipulation of independent variables and the assignment of subjects, but can specify data collecton in terms of when and from whom.

The purpose of the design is to provide a structure for assessing the effects of a treatment, or different treatments, on a sample representative of the population of interest. Normally more than one group will be used. In a simple design one group could be used as a control and left without treatment against another group to whom the treatment is administered. In more complex designs involving multiple treatments, a considerable number of groups may be required. The difference between these groups in the resulting dependent variable is termed *between-group variance*. Before the experiment commences this between-group variance needs to be at a minimum, as does the *within-group variance* (i.e. the differences between individuals within each group). The role of the design is to increase between-group variance as a result of the experimental treatments, and to keep within-group variance at a minimum.

An excellent summary of some of the problems associated with experimentation in the distribution context may be found in Doyle & Gidengil [1].

Summary

In this chapter we have attempted an overview of some of the ways in which the effects of customer service may be evaluated. The methods described should not be seen as alternatives but rather as complementary devices. Thus the need to maintain a customer service audit still exists even though each aspect of our customer service policy may have been carefully researched.

Because customer service is so important, both in terms of costs and in terms of revenue-generation potential, it is essential that the firm takes its evaluation seriously. In effect we should be just as concerned with the impact of spending money on distribution as we are on the impact of, say, advertising expenditure.

References

1 Doyle, P., and Gidengil, B.Z., 'A Review of In-Store Experiments' *Journal of Retailing,* Vol.53 No.2 Summer 1977
2 Heskett, J.L., N.A. Glaskowsky and K.M. Ivie, *Business Logistics,* Ronald Press, 1973
3 Perrault, W.D., and Russ, F.A., 'Improving Physical Distribution Service Decisions with Trade-Off Analysis' *International Journal of Physical Distribution* Vol.7 No.3 1977

10   Customer service: an overview

A key theme of this book has been that a firm's physical distribution activity should not just be seen as the means of moving goods from factory or depot to the customer but rather that it provides the means of creating *availability*. Availability should be viewed as the output of the physical distribution system and, in essence, is what customer service is all about — 'the right product in the right place at the right time'. As we have already noted there are many facets to customer service but in the end the totality of this service is satisfied demand.

For any company intent upon improving its market position through distribution a prerequisite is to focus upon the *output* of its distributive activities rather than to concentrate, as so many firms do, upon the *inputs*. Concern solely with inputs leads to over-emphasis on cost reduction without regard for the resulting impacts on the market place. Customer service can be looked upon as a vital element in the company's marketing mix. Indeed, as we shall see, there is strong evidence to suggest that in many markets customer service can be a stronger influence upon purchase behaviour than, say, advertising or price. Put at its simplest, if the product is not on the shelf when the customer wants it, then even the strongest brand-loyalty may be overcome.

Given the potency of availability as a marketing weapon it is perhaps surprising therefore that it has not been given more attention. Many companies will devote much time to weighing the efficiency of their advertising budget and yet will give only passing consideration to the efficiency of their customer service offering — even though they will probably spend many times more money in a single year on distribution than they will on advertising.

Customer service must be examined from a number of perspectives if it is to play its full role in the company's marketing effort. First, it must be seen in both strategic and tactical terms. Second, it must be looked at from the point of view of cost-effectiveness. The strategic issue concerns the building of long-term customer relationships whilst the tactical aspect is directed to the gaining of short-term marketing advantage. Cost-effectiveness analysis is a prerequisite when the company is weighing up the advantages of spending money on customer service in comparison with other uses of its resources. Given these considerations, there will emerge a number of options for the company, a number of ways in which the various elements of customer service may best be assembled for a given marketing situation.

Each of these issues is worthy of further consideration.

The strategic and tactical impact of customer service

An ever-present problem for the marketing man is the estimation of the longer-term effects of his tactical decisions. For example, will a series of promotional price-cuts lead to an eventual erosion of the brand's 'value' in the consumer's eyes, even though short-term sales might be boosted? Or will the launch of a new product lead over time to a 'cannibalisation' of our existing brands?

The same sort of problems arise in customer service decisions. Availability and the other associated elements of customer service can have both a short- and a long-term effect. In the case of products that are 'critical' to the would-be purchaser in the sense that they are vital to his immediate purpose (e.g. a replacement cylinder-head gasket for a motorcar or a drill bit on an oil rig) then the short-term effect is obvious. If substitutes are available, then in cases like these customer service is all-important. The longer-term effects of customer service may, however, be more difficult to gauge. For example, what will be the effect on longer-term customer preference for our brand if he experiences a number of short-term service failures?

At its most basic, we might consider the 'availability' that distribution produces as providing a necessary, although not sufficient, condition for purchase — if the brand is not on the shelf then it will not be purchased, at least in that time-period. But the impact of availability can go far beyond this elemental effect by influencing longer-term customer attitudes and behaviour towards the brand and/or the store in which it is sought.

That overall sales volume is influenced by the level of distribution in terms of the number of outlets stocking the brand has been demonstrated by a number of researchers. Nuttall [8] in an early paper described the nature of this relationship for certain confectionery lines and provided a means for estimating the 'elasticity' of response to improved distribution coverage. Handyside and Irons [5] more recently have also shown that volume sales are directly related to the level of distribution penetration among retail outlets.

What is less understood however is how customer service affects the development of long-term sales relationships between buyer and seller — in other words, brand and store loyalty.

A considerable literature has built up around the subject of brand loyalty, much of it devoted to developing mathematical and/or statistical models of consumer purchase sequences. Farley and Kuehn [4] provide a useful summary of those approaches that might best be described as 'stochastic' in the sense that they purport to demonstrate how the probabilty of purchase changes as a function of past purchase behaviour. Ehrenberg [2] on the other hand has determined a number of relationships underlying repreat-buying behaviour from empirical observation; these relationships seem to hold good for all products so far examined. At the other extreme is a vast and growing literature on consumer choice behaviour in which innumerable models and theories are advanced but in which empirical evidence tends to take a back seat. Howard and Sheth [6] have perhaps provided one of the best examples of this approach in recent years.

However, only rarely in all the discussions of the question of brand loyalty does the issue of *availability* appear. One commentator, Farley [3], who has recognised the importance of such factors in this context argues that availability directs preferences towards products that are accessible to the consumer in the market — 'the supply structure rather than consumer preferences tend to dominate the brand structure'. Thus the suggestion is that within the store the customer will limit his or her choice to the products available.

As Schary and Becker [9] point out, the most obvious example of availability operating as a positive stimulus is that of impulse buying, where the customer enters a store without an observable predisposition to purchase a product and yet makes the purchase. The motivation is presumed to come from in-store stimuli, including the actual availability of the product. In effect the physical presence of the product acts as a 'memory-jerker', and this is confirmed by Kollatt and Willett [7].

One further piece of evidence worth citing in this context is the research findings of Dommermuth and Cundiff [1] who suggest that customer search patterns tend to be confined to relatively small sets of stores as alternatives and, importantly, the customer tends to make the product-choice decision within the constraints of the store's own assortments. If, as seems likely, the customer builds up shopping patterns over time, then the evidence seems to suggest that he or she is *store loyal* first and only brand loyal second.

On the face of it therefore there is strong *a priori* evidence to suggest the importance of physical availability as a key determinant of sales and hence of corporate profitability.

The customer service mission

We have already stressed the need for distribution management to identify more clearly the *outputs* of the customer service activities rather than to concentrate solely on the inputs or resources utilised in the provision of customer service.

A useful concept here is the idea of the customer service 'mission'. In the context of distribution, a mission is a set of goals to be achieved by the system within a specific product/ market context. Thus missions could be defined in terms of the nature of the market to be served, by which products and within what constraints of service and cost. A mission by its very nature cuts across traditional company lines. The successful achievement of the mission goals involves inputs from a large number of functional areas and activity centres within the firm.

Our interest in this cross-company approach in the context of customer service strategies stems from an acknowledgement that in order to achieve a desired output in customer service terms, a mix of inputs from different functional areas are required. Figure 10.1 gives the example of how one paint manufacturer identified four customer service missions, each with distinct customer service needs.

In order that the differing service needs of each mission can be met in the most cost-effective way, the right balance of inputs must be devised. Clearly a prime requirement is that at the outset the missions and their objectives must be defined and also the cost constraints within which they must be achieved. Only by establishing a framework such as this will it be possible to structure the company's operations around the goal of cost-effective customer service provision.

Our research has tended to suggest that very few companies have clearly-defined policies relating to customer service, and even fewer have taken a 'missions' view of their business, and yet in those situations where companies have taken customer service seriously then there can be significant pay-offs.

Figure 10.1 Customer service mission

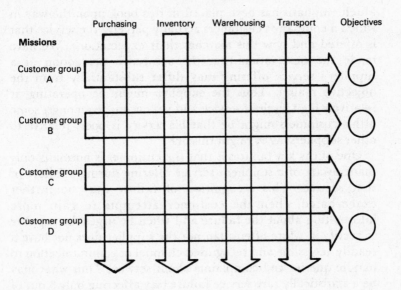

Key:

Customer group A:	The domestic consumer — a 'consumer service mission'
Customer group B:	Hospitals, schools and similar organisations — an 'institutional service mission'
Customer group C:	Contractors and other trade users — a 'professional user service mission'
Customer group D:	Supermarket chains for whom 'own brands' are manufactured — an 'own-brand service mission'

The expectations and perceptions of customers

Much emphasis has been placed in this book upon the way in which a company's customers actually perceive the service that is offered and how this matches their expectations. We have made the observation that the subjective perception of a supplier's service offering may differ substantially from the objective reality. Thus the supplier might be operating at relatively high levels of service and yet his image amongst some of his customers might be that his service is poor, relative to other suppliers. Why might this be?

One of the key failures is that the customer is normally only made aware of a supplier's service offering during a failure of that service. This recognition of failure may be further exacerbated when the customer attempts to gain more information about the failure and when he urges the supplier to rectify it. More often than not the supplier does not have a readily accessible and recognised channel of communication to handle queries and complaints about service. Thus what may be a statistically rare service failure (say affecting only 3 out of every 100 orders) becomes a problem of some magnitude in the eyes of the customer.

A further factor is also at work here. If a supplier offers a range of items with, say, an average of 97 per cent availability from stock, then it is worth remembering that, if a customer orders 10 different items from that supplier, the probability of the customer receiving the complete order from stock would drop to approximately 74 per cent, (i.e. $97\%^{10}$).

For the supplier who wishes to balance the potential savings in cost through lower service levels against the loss of customer goodwill there is a requirement to develop a policy towards service failures. This entails a recognition that, statistically, service failures will happen on a known proportion of orders. However, when these failures occur there is a managed response. Thus the supplier, for example, will inform the customer of the service failure, detailing the nature of the failure and the steps that are being taken to remedy it, the contact for queries, and the date by which the failure will be rectified.

As our studies have indicated, many of the problems in customer service arise through lack of communication between customer and supplier. Part of any policy towards customer service should be a mechanism for managing the service failure. The idea of a 'Customer Service manager' or coordinator is finding considerable acceptance these days as more and more companies recognise the importance of customer service in developing profitables sales relationships.

The appointment of such a manager should also be accompanied by a listing of all the points of contact between the company and its customers that could be regarded as having a service dimension. Thus we would include order processing, customer complaints, stock availability levels, delivery frequency, and so on. These and any other features so identified would be coordinated and monitored by the Customer Service manager. He or she would be the focus through which all of the elements of customer service would be regulated and shaped into a positive marketing tool. Our observations have tended to suggest that in many companies the diversity of customer service elements are not brought together in any cohesive way and so there is a subsequent marked loss of marketing effectiveness.

The management of the service failure is as important as the management of the routine service offering. It is the only means whereby service levels that are perceptibly lower than the competition's may be effectively countered. The strengthening of the link between customer and supplier that can result through improved communications can be considerable and after all, in the last resort, customer service is only about communications.

Conclusions

Our purpose in gathering evidence on the role of customer service in distribution strategy has been to focus upon the great potential that it has for improving marketing performance.

Whilst emphasising the strategic, i.e. longer-term, importance of customer service we have also distinguished its tactical importance in gaining immediate marketing advantage. If only to capitalise upon this potential, there is a vital requirement for a planned approach to customer service as a co-orientated element in the firm's marketing effort.

First, this requires a recognition that customer service is an inherent element in the product itself; the product has no value to the customer without the time and place utility imparted by the 'availability' that the distribution function provides. Seen from this viewpoint customer service is a value-adding component to the product rather than a source of additional cost. The evidence from our company studies, diverse though they were, all pointed in this direction; in other words, customers were more favourably disposed to suppliers whose products had recognisable customer service components.

Second, the company should redefine its marketing and distribution activity in terms of clearly-defined customer service 'missions'. Such definition leads to a greater realisation of the relative costs and benefits of alternative customer service strategies. Distribution as an activity can become more cost-effective if service objectives are delineated and the cost consequences understood. The adoption of a missions approach also has the great benefit of making the firm more conscious of the outputs of its marketing activity as well as the functional inputs necessary to achieve its service objectives.

Third, a major message of our findings has been that the future of customer service management must lie in developing stronger inter-organisational links. The bond between supplier and customer can be considerably strengthened, as we have seen, by a greater attention paid to shaping the customer service offering to meet the needs of the customer as well as the requirements of the supplier. Taking a systems view of the distribution acitivity can only lead to such conclusions; simply put, the output of the suppliers' system is the input of the customers' system.

Finally, each of the customer service systems that we have examined has led us to believe even more strongly that there is tremendous scope in all sectors of industry for developing a planned approach to distribution strategy that is based upon a carefully researched assessment of marketing reaction to customer service. This is a message that we believe will be acted upon more and more by the growing number of companies who have recognised the under-utilised power of customer service.

References

1 Dommermuth, W.P. & Cundiff, E.W., 'Shopping Goals, Shopping Centres and Selling Strategies' *Journal of Marketing* Vol.31 Oct. 1967

2 Ehrenberg, A.S.C. *Repeat Buying, Theory & Application* North Holland Publishing Co. 1972

3 Farley, J.U., 'Why does Brand Loyalty vary over Products?' *Journal of Marketing Research* Vol 1 August 1964

4 Farley, J.U., & Kuehn, A.E., 'Stochastic Models of Brand Switching' in Schwartz, G. (ed) *Science in Marketing* Wiley 1965

5 Handyside, A.J. & Irons, P.S., 'The trade as a consumer — a manufacturer's application of penetration and repeat purchase' *Journal of Marketing Research Society* Vol. 19 No. 3 1977

6 Howard, J.A. & Sheth, J.N. *The Theory of Buyer Behaviour* Wiley 1969

7 Kollatt, D.T. & Willett, R.P. 'Customers' Impulse Purchasing Behaviour' *Journal of Marketing Research* Vol.4 February 1967

8 Nuttall, C., 'The Relationship between Sales and Distribution of Certain Confectionery Lines' *Commentary* (Journal of Market Research Society) Vol VII No.4 October 1965

9 Schary, P.B. & Becker, B.W., 'The Marketing/Logistics Interface' *International Journal of Physical Distribution* Vol 3. No.4 1973

Index